Mercer Moments
in American History

Slavery 101

KEN MERCER

WESTBOW
PRESS®
A DIVISION OF THOMAS NELSON
& ZONDERVAN

WestBow Press books may be ordered through booksellers or by contacting:

WestBow Press
A Division of Thomas Nelson & Zondervan
1663 Liberty Drive
Bloomington, IN 47403
www.westbowpress.com
844-714-3454

ISBN: 978-1-6642-2513-8 (sc)
ISBN: 978-1-6642-2514-5 (hc)
ISBN: 978-1-6642-2512-1 (e)

Library of Congress Control Number: 2021903695

Print information available on the last page.

WestBow Press rev. date: 05/06/2021

Contents

Contents

Dedication

To Rosalia, my "Proverbs 31" Wife,

To my daughters, and son-in-law
Who each have a rock-solid heart for God,

To my first grandchild, a true gift from God,

To my wonderful extended family,

To the Christian pastors, speakers, commentators, and leaders
who each day influence so many of my "journeys,"

And to all the "Ephesian 6" warriors who every morning
put on their "full armor of God" to reach out to me and
many, many others with their honest love of Jesus,

**I believe the greatest gift you can ever leave
is to simply make a difference.**

This first book is dedicated to you.

Introduction

The Test

This introduction follows the unique style of my books. Your introduction is actually a multiple-choice test.

Can you pass this twenty-question test on Slavery 101?

The answer to question I is found in chapter 1, question II is in chapter 2, up to question XX being chapter 20.

I. The Declaration

The 1776 Declaration of Independence, written primarily by Thomas Jefferson, included a long list of grievances against King George III of England.

Question: Which grievance did the Southern colonies demand be deleted before they would agree to ratify the Declaration of Independence?

a) Denying trial by jury
b) Bringing slaves from Africa
c) Imposing taxes without representation
d) Quartering of British troops

II. In the Beginning

There are powerful groups pushing a revisionist history that slavery in the world began in the year 1619, and slavery was invented by the original thirteen colonies of what became the United States of America.

Question: When did slavery begin in the world?

A. AD 1619
B. AD 700
C. 1450 BC
D. More than 8,000 years ago

III. The Great Compromise of 1787

During the first Constitutional Convention of 1787, the representation for each state proved to be the most controversial issue.[1]

The resolution for this issue was the Great Compromise (aka the Connecticut Compromise), which later in the convention would bring into question the counting of slaves in Southern states for representation.

Question: What are the key elements of the Great Compromise?

a) The Senate will be comprised of two senators from each state.
b) The House of Representatives will have the number of members allocated according to each state's population.
c) Both of the above.
d) None of the above.

---

[1] https://www.history.com/news/how-the-great-compromise-affects-politics-today.

IV. The Three-Fifths Compromise

Another major dispute arose in the Constitutional Convention of 1787 regarding the counting of the slave population of Southern states in allocating members for the new US House of Representatives.[2]

Northern antislavery states were shocked when the Southern states wanted to count 100 percent of the slave population to create greater congressional representation. Northern states believed it unfair count slaves who had no rights in the South. Heated debate resulted in the famous "Three-Fifths Compromise."

Question: During the 1787 Constitutional Convention, why did the Southern states want to count 100 percent of their slaves?

   a) The Southern states wanted to increase their power in the US House to have the votes to abolish slavery eventually.
   b) The Southern states wanted to increase their power in the US House to have the voting strength to provide for the education of the children of slaves.
   c) The Southern states wanted to increase their representation in the US House to have votes to allow slaves the right to own property and to vote.
   d) The Southern states wanted to increase their power in the US House to block any future attempt by the Northern states to end the expansion of or to abolish slavery.

---

[2] https://www.britannica.com/topic/three-fifths-compromise.

V. First State to Outlaw Slavery

In 1807, Congress passed legislation to outlaw the importation of African slaves. The law was signed by President Thomas Jefferson. Prior to 1807, some states had already outlawed the importation of new slaves and abolished slavery altogether.[3]

Question: Which was (were) the first state(s) to outlaw slavery?

a) Massachusetts
b) Pennsylvania
c) New York
d) Vermont
e) Vermont and Pennsylvania

VI. Amazing Grace

In 1833, the British Parliament honored a man for his Christian leadership in the passage of the 1807 law to abolish the slave trade and the 1833 law to abolish all slavery in the United Kingdom.[4,5] Parliament resolved to bury this man in Westminster Abbey.

Question: Who was this man who, beginning in the late 1780s, persevered for over forty years to abolish slavery in the United Kingdom?

A) William Pitt
B) King George III
C) William Wilberforce
D) John Newton

---

[3] https://www.history.com/this-day-in-history/congress-abolishes-the-african-slave-trade.

[4] https://www.westminster-abbey.org/abbey-commemorations/commemorations/william-wilberforce-family.

[5] http://origins.osu.edu/review/after-abolition-britain-and-slave-trade-1807.

VII. First Nation to Abolish Slavery

Today, in the twenty-first century, there is much righteous indignation from politicians regarding who to blame for slavery and who should pay any financial reparations to the impacted nations and descendants of slaves. One good starting point might be to study the who, how, and when the world determined to abolish slavery.

Question: Which was the first country (nation, republic, state) to abolish slavery?

    a) United Kingdom (Britain)
    b) United States
    c) A country in Africa
    d) A country in Asia
    e) Vermont Republic

VIII. The Gag Rule

A "gag rule" is a parliamentary procedure used by members of decision-making bodies in which they agree to limit—or "table"—the introduction, consideration, or discussion of a usually controversial topic.

The most famous gag rule began with the 1836 Congress's attempt to prevent the discussion and debate of slavery.[6]

Question: Who was the main target of the 1836–1844 series of gag rules in the House of Representatives?

    A) John Quincy Adams
    B) President Andrew Jackson
    C) Rep. Henry Pinckney, South Carolina
    D) John Hammond, South Carolina

---

[6] https://www.britannica.com/topic/gag-rule

IX. Percentage of Slaves Transported to the United States

The transatlantic slave trade documented the purchase of 12.5 million Africans from their captors, the dominant and powerful African and Arab-Muslim tribes.[7]

It is estimated that 10.7 million of these new slaves survived the trip from Africa across the Atlantic Ocean to the "New World" of North America, the Caribbean, and South America.

Question: What percentage of those 10.7 million African slaves were transported to the thirteen colonies of what became the United States?

a. 75 percent
b. 5 percent or less
c. 25 percent
d. 50 percent

X. 1857 Dred Scott Decision

In the famous 1857 Dred Scott decision, the Southern-influenced US Supreme Court ruled that African Americans, whether free or enslaved, were not citizens, and that the Missouri Compromise, which was meant to balance the admittance of free and slave states, was unconstitutional.[8]

The 1857 Dred Scott decision was overturned by which constitutional amendment(s)?

A) Thirteenth Amendment
B) Fourteenth Amendment
C) Fifteenth Amendment
D) Thirteen and Fourteenth Amendments
E) None of the above; the Dred Scott decision was never overturned.

---

[7] http://slaveryandremembrance.org/articles/article/?id=A0002.
[8] https://www.britannica.com/event/Dred-Scott-decision.

XI. Republican Slaves?

The 1860 US Census determined the population of the United States to be 31.4 million persons. This included 3.95 million slaves.[9]

Question: In 1860, what percentage of slaves were owned by Republicans?

a) 42 percent
b) 31 percent
c) 19.3 percent
d) Far fewer than 1 percent

XII. Moses of the Underground Railroad

Moses is known as the great leader, lawgiver, and prophet who led the Hebrew people from slavery in Egypt to freedom in the Promised Land.

The Underground Railroad also had a Moses who led African American slaves to freedom.

Question: Which person listed below was known as the "Moses" of the Underground Railroad?

A. Frederick Douglass
B. Crispus Attucks
C. Wentworth Cheswell
D. Harriett Tubman

---

[9] https://www.census.gov/library/publications/1864/dec/1860a.html.

XIII. First African American Medal of Honor Recipient

The Medal of Honor is the highest military award presented by the United States to a member of our armed forces. Recipients distinguished themselves by risking their own lives above and beyond the call of duty in action against an enemy of the United States.

Question: Who was the first African American recipient of the Medal of Honor?

a) First Sergeant Alexander Kelly
b) Corporal Decatur Dorsey
c) Private Charles Veal
d) Sergeant William Carney

XIV. The Thirteenth Amendment

On January 31, 1865, the US House passed the Thirteenth Amendment to abolish slavery. All eighty-six Republicans voted for passage.[10]

Question: In 1865, how many of the sixty-five Democrats in the US House voted for the Thirteenth Amendment?

a) Only fifteen
b) Over half of the sixty-five
c) All sixty-five
d) None

MMAH Note: Amendments to our US Constitution require passage by a two-thirds majority in both the Senate and House before sending to the states for ratification. Then the process requires three-fourths of the states to ratify the amendment before it becomes law.

---

[10] https://www.govtrack.us/congress/votes/38-2/h480

XV. The Fifteenth Amendment

In 1870, the Fifteenth Amendment to our US Constitution, which granted African American men the right to vote, was adopted.[11] For passage, a constitutional amendment required two-thirds of the members of both the US House and Senate to vote, "Aye."

What percentage of Democrats in the US House and Senate voted for the Fifteenth Amendment?

a) None
b) 50 percent in the House and 60 percent in the Senate
c) 60 percent in the House and 75 percent in the Senate
d) 70 percent in the House and 100 percent in the Senate

XVI. First African American Member of Congress

Question: Who was the first African American to serve in the US Congress?

a) Tim Scott, South Carolina, Republican
b) Rev. Hiram Rhodes Revels, Mississippi, Republican
c) Blanche Bruce, Mississippi, Republican
d) Edward Brook, Massachusetts. Republican

---

[11] https://www.history.com/topics/black-history/fifteenth-amendment.

XVII. Arab-Muslim Slave Trade

Transatlantic slave trade and the Arab-Muslim slave trade each targeted the capturing, buying, and selling of slaves. However, little is known and discussed about the Arab-Muslim slave trade.

Question: Which statement is true regarding the Arab-Muslim slave trade?

The Arab-Muslim slave trade:

a) Is taught and widely discussed in the schools, colleges, and universities of the United States.
b) Captured, bought, and sold fewer slaves than the thirteen colonies.
c) Did not target female slaves.
d) Did not include white slavery.
e) Was a much more humane form of slavery.
f) All the above are false statements.

XVIII. Last Nation to Abolish Slavery

Great Britain abolished the Atlantic slave trade" in 1807 and in all British colonies in 1833. The United States abolished slavery in 1865 with Lincoln's Emancipation Proclamation and the states' ratification of the Thirteenth Amendment to our constitution.

Question: What was the last nation to abolish, at least on paper, the practice of slavery?

a) Mauritania
b) Saudi Arabia
c) Yemen
d) Qatar
e) United Arab Emirates (UAE)

XIX. Worst and Best in the Twenty-First Century

In 2018, the highest documented rates of human slavery continue to remain in countries on the continents of Africa and Asia.

Question: Which country has the highest rate (human slaves per thousand population) of slavery in the world?

a) Eritrea, Africa
b) Sudan, Africa
c) Burundi, Africa
d) Iran
e) North Korea
f) Democrat Republic of the Congo, Africa

XX. First "Civil Rights President"

In the nineteenth and twentieth centuries, several landmark pieces of civil rights legislation were passed.

Who was considered the first "civil rights" president?

a) Sixteenth president—Abraham Lincoln
b) Seventeenth president—Andrew Johnson
c) Thirty-sixth president—Lyndon B. Johnson
d) Eighteenth president—Ulysses S. Grant

Recently you repented
and did what is right in my sight:
Each of you proclaimed freedom
to your own people.
You even made a covenant before me
in the house that bears my Name.

—Jeremiah 34:15 NIV

1

The Declaration

The 1776 Declaration of Independence, primarily written by Thomas Jefferson, included a long list of grievances against King George III of England.

Question: Which grievance did the Southern colonies demand be deleted before they would agree to ratify the Declaration of Independence?

a) Denying trial by jury
b) Bringing slaves from Africa
c) Imposing taxes without representation
d) Quartering of British troops

The unanimous Declaration of the thirteen united States of America.

I grew up believing the famous Declaration of Independence was unanimously approved by the colonies. Not true.

The document delineated the reasons for declaring independence, a list of grievances or complaints against King George III. But the colonies had to agree to all the grievances before passage of the final document.

Remember that this is the Jefferson who inspired the world with his famous pronouncement that "all men are created equal" and the profound trilogy of "inalienable rights" being "life, liberty and the pursuit of happiness."[12], [13]

Here is the political paradox: Jefferson was a slave owner.

Jefferson inherited slaves from his father in 1768 and acquired slaves on his marriage in 1773. He owned an average of two hundred slaves at any point in time.[14]

Yet historical records prove his original draft of the Declaration of Independence included a grievance that blamed King George III for bringing slavery to the thirteen colonies.[15]

Thomas Jefferson, a lifelong slave owner, called slavery a violation of the, "most sacred rights of life & liberty." Jefferson blamed King George III for creating a, "market where MEN should be bought & sold."[16]

It is my hope to inspire and challenge my readers to dive deeper. Please note that slavery existed in the world for more than eight thousand years *before* the 1776 founding of the United States. Before the Declaration of Independence in 1776, not one nation had ever moved to abolish slavery.

---

[12] https://www.history.com/topics/us-presidents/thomas-jefferson.
[13] https://www.britannica.com/biography/Thomas-Jefferson/Slavery-and-racism.
[14] https://www.history.com/topics/us-presidents/thomas-jefferson.
[15] https://teachingamericanhistory.org/library/document/rough-draft-of-the-declaration-of-independence/.
[16] https://teachingamericanhistory.org/library/document/rough-draft-of-the-declaration-of-independence/.

SIGNING THE DECLARATION OF AMERICAN INDEPENDENCE.

Obviously, Jefferson's grievance on slavery was one of the most intense debates over the adoption of the Declaration of Independence. To ensure agreement of the Southern colonies, Jefferson's grievance on slavery was ultimately deleted by the delegates in Philadelphia for the 1776 Continental Congress.

This appears to be self-contradictory. Thomas Jefferson, who owned an average of two hundred slaves during his lifetime, was prepared to begin our United States of America by publicly declaring in our founding document that slavery was evil.

What could have so radically changed the hearts and minds of men regarding slavery?

I passionately believe the difference between the thirteen British colonies and the rest of the proslavery world was the wave of spiritual revival in America known as the "Great Awakening." The message of freedom and recognition of sins had a profound effect on our founders and led to the establishment of many American societies to abolish slavery. For example, in 1785, the first chief justice of the United States, John Jay, founded the first abolition society in New York. In 1799, Jay, who had become governor of New York, signed into law an act for the gradual abolition of slavery—sixty years before the Civil War.[17]

_____

_____

Answer: The correct answer to the question at the beginning of this *Mercer Moment in American History* is B.

Please review Jefferson's entire original grievance on slavery that delegates from the Southern colonies wanted removed before agreeing to the final twenty-seven grievances of the Declaration of Independence.

---

[17] http://www.columbia.edu/cu/libraries/inside/dev/jay/JaySlavery.html.

He has waged cruel war against human nature itself, violating its most sacred rights of life & liberty in the persons of a distant people who never offended him, captivating & carrying them into slavery in another hemisphere,

or to incur miserable death in their transportation thither. this piratical warfare, the opprobrium of infidel powers, is the warfare of the CHRISTIAN king of Great Britain.

determined to keep open a market where MEN should be bought & sold,

he has prostituted his negative for suppressing every legislative attempt to prohibit or to restrain this execrable commerce:

and that this assemblage of horrors might want no fact of distinguished die,

he is now exciting those very people to rise in arms among us, and to purchase that liberty of which he has deprived them, by murdering the people upon whom he also obtruded them;

thus paying off former crimes committed against the liberties of one people, with crimes which he urges them to commit against the lives of another.

In days to come,
when your son asks you,
"What does this mean?"
say to him,
"With a mighty hand the Lord brought us out of Egypt,
out of the land of slavery."

—Exodus 13:14 NIV

2

In the Beginning

There are powerful groups pushing a revisionist history that slavery in the world began in the year 1619, and slavery was invented by the original thirteen colonies of what became the United States of America.

Question: When did slavery begin in the world?

a) AD 1619
b) AD 700
c) 1450 BC
d) More than eight thousand years ago

As a Christian, I believe you should fight hard but only fight with truth. However, I learned that for those who oppose Judeo-Christian values, truth is not a requirement.

In the goal to end worldwide slavery, the conversations must all be founded on truth, not on a political agenda. Truth must be our requirement.

Joseph Goebbels was Adolph Hitler's Nazi minister of propaganda.[18] The Nazis were the National Socialist Party of Germany.[19] The goal of the Nazis was to create one centralized, big government that controlled all banking and finance, religion, education, business, and journalism.

---

[18] https://www.britannica.com/biography/Joseph-Goebbels.
[19] https://www.history.com/topics/world-war-ii/joseph-goebbels.

Goebbels believed in controlling the "messaging" to all citizens. Allow me to summarize the philosophy and method of implementing the plan of the official Nazi minister of propaganda.

> Tell a lie. Use our media to repeat that lie. Teach and keep repeating that lie in our Nazi-controlled schools and in our churches. Then one day, that lie will be perceived as truth.

The Nazis had a "master plan" that required the slave labor of millions of Jews. The implementation of that plan was the "final solution"—the Holocaust—in which more than 6 million Jewish children, women, and men were murdered.[20],[21]

I opened this chapter with the Nazi minister of propaganda for a reason.

Many American university students are currently fed a two-pronged regimen of propaganda:

1) Slavery is a unique American phenomenon.
2) In the year 1619, slavery in the world began in the thirteen colonies that became the United States.

In 2019, Tom Lindsay, an expert in higher-education policy, pointed to the alarming results of a published eleven-year study of what college students knew about American history.

> Students overwhelmingly believe that slavery, "was an American problem ... and they are very fuzzy about the history of slavery prior to the Colonial era. Their entire education about slavery was confined to America."[22]

---

[20] https://www.debate.org/opinions/which-is-worse-slavery-yes-or-the-holocaust-no.
[21] https://encyclopedia.ushmm.org/content/en/article/forced-labor-an-overview.
[22] https://www.forbes.com/sites/tomlindsay/2019/08/30/after-all-didnt-america-invent-slavery/#3e1321037ef6.

In 2020, we began hearing that leading socialist educators were promoting an agenda that teaches students the birth of our nation was not the year 1776 but 1619.[23]

Most historians agree that 1619 is the year that slavery began in British North America, our thirteen colonies. Honest experts will acknowledge that slavery was not invented in 1619.

We know that before Columbus, the ancient Aztecs and Mayans held slaves. There are horrific stories of mass human sacrifices to their gods, and the victims were their slaves.[24] In 1487, the opening of the Tenochtitlan Aztec temple began with the human sacrifice of 20,000 captives.[25]

Mayan slavery was definitely pre-Columbus with settlements and ruins from 1800 BC to AD 900.[26] The famous Mayan temples, palaces, and pyramids were built almost entirely by slaves between AD 250 and AD 900.[27], [28]

This means Mayan slavery—and yes, Mayan human sacrifice—occurred at least six hundred years before the arrival of Columbus to the New World in 1492.

What did happen in the British North America colonies in the year 1619?

---

[23] https://thefederalist.com/2020/08/10/8-big-takedowns-of-the-1619-project-for-its-one-year-anniversary/.

[24] http://aztec-maya-inca.weebly.com/aztec-slavery.html.

[25] https://www.ancient.eu/timeline/Aztec_Sacrifice/.

[26] https://www.history.com/topics/ancient-americas/maya

[27] https://slaveryinjustice.wordpress.com/slavery-in-ancient-aztec-mayan-and-inca/

[28] http://aztec-maya-inca.weebly.com/mayan-slavery.html

SACRIFICE ON THE TECHATL STONE.

In 1619, the Portuguese slave ship *Sao Joao Baptista* was transporting 350 Angolan slaves to Vera Cruz, Mexico. The ship was attacked in the Gulf of Mexico by two English privateer ships, one being the *White Lion,* that took at least twenty slaves from the Portuguese slave ship.[29],[30] The *White Lion* was severely damaged from the battle. It sailed up the coast and then suffered more damage in a powerful storm in the Atlantic. The ship became in critical need of major repairs and supplies.

In 1619, the *White Lion* landed in the Virginia colony. In Jamestown, the *White Lion* traded twenty African slaves as agricultural workers in return for food and ship repairs.[31]

The year 1619 is important. That is the date we believe slavery was introduced to North America. But as for when slavery began and was introduced in the world, the year 1619 is the wrong answer.

In AD 700, the Arab-Muslim slave trade began, 750 years before the discovery of the New World. This was one thousand years before the Christians of the Great Awakening began worldwide movements to abolish slavery. I dedicate with diligent documentation a whole chapter near the end of this book to the Arab-Muslim slave trade.[32]

Christians and Jews remember the book of Exodus and that the Hebrews were kept in slavery for more than four hundred years by the Egyptians. Annual Passover remembrances retell the story of the Hebrew exodus from slavery to the Promised Land.[33]

---

[29] https://www.history.com/this-day-in-history/first-african-slave-ship-arrives-jamestown-colony.

[30] https://www.usatoday.com/in-depth/news/nation/2019/08/21/american-slavery-began-1619-project-documents-brutal-journey/1968793001/.

[31] https://historicjamestowne.org/history/the-first-africans/.

[32] https://atlantablackstar.com/2014/06/02/10-facts-about-the-arab-enslavement-of-black-people-not-taught-in-schools/.

[33] https://www.freetheslaves.net/take-action/faith-in-action-ending-slavery/.

The slavery of the Hebrew people occurred around 1450–1350 BC, almost three thousand years before the first African slaves were sold in Jamestown.

Answer: The correct answer to the question at the beginning of this *Mercer Moment in American History* is D.

Using multiple sources, it is safe to state that slavery began in the world more than eight thousand years ago.

Research points to slavery beginning in Mesopotamia.[34] The Sumerians, Babylonians, and Assyrians each practiced slavery, first emerging almost 9,000 years ago (6800 BC). Enemies captured in war were commonly kept by the conquering country as slaves.[35],[36]

Additional resources believe that the institution of slavery in the agriculture communities of Mesopotamia may be 8,000 to 10,000 years old.[37],[38]

So clearly, to state that slavery in the world began more than years 8,000 ago is a safe and diligently researched and supportable answer.

---

[34] https://sites.psu.edu/ancientmesopotamianwarfare/slavery/.

[35] https://www.histclo.com/act/work/slave/anc/sa-mes.html.

[36] https://www.freetheslaves.net/about-slavery/slavery-in-history/.

[37] https://newint.org/features/2001/08/05/history.

[38] http://world-history-education-resources.com/mesopotamia/slaves-mesopotamia.html.

3

The Great Compromise of 1787

During the first Constitutional Convention of 1787, the representation for each state proved to be the most controversial issue.[39]

The resolution for this issue was the Great Compromise (aka Connecticut Compromise), which later in the convention brought into question the counting of slaves in Southern states for representation.

Question: What are the key elements of the Great Compromise?

a) The Senate will be comprised of two senators from each state.
b) The House of Representatives will have the number of members according to each state's population.
c) Both of the above.
d) None of the above.

I intended this to be an easy question. However, I found that too many Americans do not share this basic understanding of the US Constitution of our constitutional federal republic.

Our form of democracy has a bicameral system that includes both the US House and the US Senate.[40]

---

[39] https://www.history.com/news/how-the-great-compromise-affects-politics-today.
[40] https://www.britannica.com/topic/Connecticut-Compromise.

Why? Heated debate in 1787 put our early country at risk. States with larger populations believed they deserved more power and thus representation based on population. States with small populations demanded equal representation.[41], [42]

Our Founding Fathers considered different options and resolved the issue with the Great Compromise. For example, would each state have one, two, or three senators? One senator for each state was not a viable compromise because if that one person was not in attendance, that state would have no representation in the Senate. Three senators for each state was discussed with the advantage of requiring a quorum, but this option would be much more costly.

The convention approved two senators for each state no matter how large or how small the state's population. However, this equal representation heavily favored the lesser-populated states.[43], [44]

The compromise came when the convention decided to include a second body, the US House of Representatives, with members for each state determined by population. This representation gives more power to the more-populated states.[45]

Answer: The correct answer to the question at the beginning of this *Mercer Moment in American History* is C.

The United States has both the Senate and the House of Representatives. This bicameral system. In the Senate, each state has two members, and

---

[41] https://www.history.com/news/how-the-great-compromise-affects-politics-today.

[42] https://historycooperative.org/great-compromise/.

[43] https://www.britannica.com/topic/Connecticut-Compromise.

[44] https://www.history.com/news/how-the-great-compromise-affects-politics-today.

[45] https://www.britannica.com/topic/Connecticut-Compromise.

in the House of Representatives, the number of each state's members is determined by population.

Again, this is our bicameral system.

"But Mr. Mercer, what does the Great Compromise have to do with the issue of slavery?"

Okay, be patient. You are now ready for the next subject: the Three-Fifths Compromise!

The Signing of The Declaration of Independence by our American Founding Fathers in Philadelphia.

4

The Three-Fifths Compromise

Another major dispute arose in the Constitutional Convention of 1787 regarding the counting of the slave population of Southern states in allocating members for the new US House of Representatives.[46]

Northern antislavery states were shocked when the Southern states wanted to count 100 percent of the slave population to create greater congressional representation. Northern states believed it unfair count slaves who had no rights in the South. Heated debate resulted in the famous "Three-Fifths Compromise."

Question: During the 1787 Constitutional Convention, why did the Southern states want to count 100 percent of their slaves?

a) The Southern states wanted to increase their power in the US House to have the votes to abolish slavery eventually.

b) The Southern states wanted to increase their power in the US House to have the voting strength to provide for the education of the children of slaves.

c) The Southern states wanted to increase their representation in the US House to have votes to allow slaves the right to own property and to vote.

d) The Southern states wanted to increase their power in the US House to block any future attempt from the Northern states either to end the expansion of or to abolish slavery.

---

[46] https://www.britannica.com/topic/three-fifths-compromise.

Opening Prayer of the first session of the First Continental Congress, September 5, 1774

The talking points of many modern politicians often attack our Founding Fathers as being racists who believed, "a black man only counted for three-fifths of a person." Without any historical context, their "evidence" for racism is the Three-Fifths Compromise of our original US Constitution. But when we study the Three-Fifths Compromise in its historical context, we gain a completely different understanding.[47]

The 1787 Constitution stated that "Three fifths of all other Persons" would count toward representation for the Southern states.[48]

For a current context, in the 2010 Census, the United States had a population of 310 million. With a fixed number of 435 members of our House of Representatives, a state would be allocated by one member for approximately every 710,000 residents.[49],[50] While each state has two US senators, by law each state is promised at least one member of the House.

There are seven states that have only one Member of the US House: Alaska, Delaware, Montana, North Dakota, South Dakota, Vermont, and Wyoming.[51]

As we found in the Great Compromise, the more populous states enjoy greater representation and thus have more power in the US House.[52]

In today's twenty-first century, many are raising the issue of citizens vs. noncitizens when it comes to the population for determining the representation of border states.

For example, California has 3.6 million noncitizens (legal permanent residents) and 2.4 million undocumented immigrants. Many argue the "fairness" of these six million noncitizens providing California with eight

47 https://www.theusconstitution.org/news/understanding-the-three-fifths-compromise/.
48 https://constitution.laws.com/three-fifths-compromise.
49 https://history.house.gov/Historical-Highlights/1901-1950/The-Permanent-Apportionment-Act-of-1929/.
50 https://www.house.gov/representatives.
51 https://www.house.gov/the-house-explained.
52 https://constitution.laws.com/three-fifths-compromise.

or more additional members in the House of Representatives. However, the law in our US Constitution counts everyone. And as a matter of historical context, the Three-Fifths Compromise of 1787 was "fixed" in 1865 with the Fourteenth Amendment.[53]

Now what were the prevailing circumstances in 1787 and the first Constitutional Convention?

In 1787, slavery was already a huge issue. Vermont, New Hampshire, Rhode Island, Massachusetts, and Connecticut had abolished slavery. By 1804, New York and New Jersey followed suit, meaning all Northern states had outlawed slavery.

Christian groups in the North championed the abolishment of slavery. Southern slaveholders feared this new nation would bring an end to the expansion of slavery and then the eventual abolishment of slavery.

When the population counts were reported by members at the Constitutional Convention, the members from the Northern states were astonished. The numbers from the Southern states seemed to be inflated because they included almost 700,000 slaves. The South included 100 percent of their slaves to increase representation and power in the House.[54]

Imagine the moral and righteous indignation of the Northern abolitionists.

The South did not allow slaves the right to own property, vote, run for office, or enjoy the fruits of their labor. It was illegal to teach children of slaves to read and write. But ironically, the South wanted to count slaves as a way to better represent them.

The compromise to preserve this fragile new nation was to count only 60 percent, or three fifths of the slave population. This still gave the South about 30 percent to 35 percent more representation in the US House.[55]

---

[53] https://constitution.laws.com/three-fifths-compromise.

[54] https://www.theusconstitution.org/news/understanding-the-three-fifths-compromise/.

[55] https://constitution.laws.com/three-fifths-compromise.

Here is the irony. The Three-Fifths Compromise was never a racist statement of our Founding Fathers. It was a tactic used by the Northern antislave states to limit the power of racists whose plan was to continue and even expand slavery.

_____

_____

Answer: The correct answer to the question at the beginning of this *Mercer Moment in American History* is D.

The Southern states wanted to increase their power in the US House to block any future attempts from the Northern states to either end the expansion of slavery or to abolish slavery.

Of all the tragic facts
about the history of slavery,
the most astonishing to an American today is that,
although slavery was a worldwide institution
for thousands of years,
nowhere in the world
was slavery a controversial issue
prior to the 18th century.[56]

—Dr. Thomas Sowell

---

[56] https://www.right-mind.us/thomas-sowell-on-slavery-and-this-fact-there-are-more-slaves-today-than-were-seized-from-africa-in-four-centuries/.

5

First State to Outlaw Slavery

In 1807, Congress passed legislation to outlaw the importation of African slaves. The law was signed by President Thomas Jefferson. Prior to 1807, some states had already outlawed the importation of new slaves and abolished slavery altogether.[57]

Question: Which was (were) the first state(s) to outlaw slavery?

a) Massachusetts
b) Pennsylvania
c) New York
d) Vermont
e) Vermont and Pennsylvania

Article 1 of the Constitution deals with the legislative branch. In section 9, our founders included this often overlooked and obscure item regarding the year (prior to 1807) to end the importation of persons:

> The Migration or Importation of such Persons as any
> of the States now existing shall think proper to admit,
> shall not be prohibited by the Congress prior to the Year
> one thousand eight hundred and eight, but a tax or duty

[57] https://www.history.com/this-day-in-history/congress-abolishes-the-african-slave-trade.

28

may be imposed on such Importation, not exceeding ten
dollars for each Person.[58]

Clearly this clause relates to the international or transatlantic slave trade.

The founders strategically placed this device in our Constitution to end the importation of slaves throughout all the states beginning after the twentieth year of our Constitution.

After the adoption of the Constitution in 1787, section 9 prohibited Congress from any legislation restricting the importation of persons. However, for the first twenty years, Congress did have the authority to levy a tax or duty of up to ten dollars per imported slave.

After twenty years from the time of adoption, the Constitution would allow Congress to write a law finally to end the importation of African slaves.

On December 2, 1806, President Thomas Jefferson, in his annual message—or State of the Union address—to Congress, called to criminalize international slave trade:

> ... withdraw the citizens of the United States from all further participation in those violations of human rights ... which the morality, the reputation, and the best of our country have long been eager to proscribe.[59]

Congress passed legislation to end the international slave trade in 1807, and President Jefferson signed it into law.

> Be it enacted by the Senate and House of Representatives
> of the United States of America in Congress assembled,

---

[58] http://americanusconstitution.com/article1section9.html#:~:text=%20%20%20
1%20Article%201%2C%20Section%209,No%20Capitation%2C%20or%20
other%20direct%2C%20Tax...%20More%20.

[59] https://www.infoplease.com/primary-sources/government/presidential-speeches/
state-union-address-thomas-jefferson-december-2-1806.

that from and after the first day of January, one thousand eight hundred and eight,

it shall not be lawful to import or bring into the United States or the territories thereof from any foreign kingdom, place, or country,

any negro, mulatto, or person of colour, with intent to hold, sell, or dispose of such negro, mulatto, or person of colour, as a slave, or to be held to service or labour.[60], [61], [62]

This critical and strategic step placed by our Founding Fathers in the 1787 Constitution would, as planned, in the year 1807 outlaw the international trade of human slaves.[63]

However, it was just the first step. In 1862, Abraham Lincoln signed his Emancipation Proclamation, declaring that of January 1, 1863, slavery would be outlawed in the Confederacy. But the domestic buying and selling of slaves within the United States remained legal until 1865, when the Union won the Civil War, and Republicans led passage of the Thirteenth Amendment to abolish slavery.

But did the first states have to wait until 1807 to abolish slavery? No!

My friend, historian David Barton of WallBuilders, reminds us that:

wide-scale abolitionism was planted by the Biblical beliefs of several early colonies.[64]

---

[60] https://www.history.com/this-day-in-history/congress-abolishes-the-african-slave-trade.

[61] https://www.politico.com/story/2018/03/02/congress-votes-to-ban-slave-importation-march-2-1807-430820.

[62] http://abolition.nypl.org/content/docs/text/Act_of_1807.pdf.

[63] https://www.history.com/this-day-in-history/congress-abolishes-the-african-slave-trade.

[64] https://wallbuilders.com/americas-exceptional-history-of-anti-slavery/.

I believe for the first time in the world one nation was finally moving to abolish slavery. Christians were rising up and putting their faith into action.

David Barton, in his outstanding argument for American exceptionalism, summarizes it best:

> By 1804, all of the New England states as well as Vermont, New York, and New Jersey had either completely abolished slavery or enacted positive laws for the gradual abolition of it.
>
> This is four years before the Federal Congress ends the slave trade, and almost three decades before England votes to follow suit and abolishes slavery.[65]

Here is a timeline of those states that abolished slavery before the end of the twenty-year requirement found in Article 1, Section 9 of our Constitution:

---

[65] https://wallbuilders.com/americas-exceptional-history-of-anti-slavery/.

Year	State	Event
1804	New Jersey	Abolishes slavery.[1]
1799	New York	Began the gradual emancipation of slaves.[2]
1784	Connecticut	Began the gradual abolition of slavery, freeing all children of slaves and then all slaves.[3]
1784	Rhode Island	A 1652 law to abolish slavery in the "Providence Plantation" began the abolition of slavery. *Note:* Some believe Rhode Island abolished slavery in 1774. My research states otherwise.[4]
1783	Massachusetts	State supreme court, referencing that state's 1781 constitution, rules slavery is unconstitutional. All slaves are immediately set free.[5]
1783	New Hampshire	Began the gradual abolition of slavery.[6]
1780	Pennsylvania	Passed laws for the gradual abolition of slavery, beginning with the future children of slaves.[7]
1777	Vermont	Abolishes slavery and even begins to offer voting rights. *Note:* In 1777 Vermont was considered an independent republic.[8,9]

[66] https://legallegacy.wordpress.com/2018/02/15/february-15-1804-new-jersey-passes-legislation-for-the-gradual-abolition-of-slavery/.

[67] http://historyinaction.columbia.edu/field-notes/slavery-and-emancipation-new-york/.

[68] https://connecticuthistory.org/topics-page/slavery-and-abolition/.

[69] http://slavenorth.com/rhodeisland.htm.

[70] http://slavenorth.com/massemancip.htm.

[71] http://slavenorth.com/newhampshire.htm.

[72] http://slavenorth.com/paemancip.htm.

[73] http://slavenorth.com/vermont.htm.

[74] https://nmaahc.si.edu/blog-post/vermont-1777-early-steps-against-slavery.

CONSTITUTION HOUSE

Windsor, settled in 1764, became the political center of the Upper Connecticut River Valley. Here the Constitution of the "Free and Independent State of Vermont" was adopted at the tavern of Elijah West on July 8, 1777. This constitution was the first to prohibit slavery and establish universal manhood suffrage. Vermont was an independent republic until 1791, when it was admitted into the Union as the 14th state.

VERMONT DIVISION FOR HISTORIC PRESERVATION 1990

Answer: The correct answer to the question at the beginning of this *Mercer Moment in American History* is E.

The best answers are Pennsylvania (1780) and Vermont (1777).

A little nuance: Most do not know that in 1777, Vermont was an independent and sovereign country. In fact, the Vermont Republic may be the first country to outlaw slavery.

Some may see this is a technicality. In 1791, Vermont joined the United States of America as our fourteenth state. In 1777 the Vermont Republic had already moved to abolish slavery; but again, Vermont was not a state until 1791.[75], [76]

Pennsylvania was one of the thirteen original colonies that formed our Union. In 1780 it moved to abolish slavery, eighty years before the Civil War.

---

[75] http://slavenorth.com/vermont.htm.
[76] https://www.vpr.org/post/history-slavery-vermont-across-new-england#stream/0.

Therefore,
since we are surrounded by such
a great cloud of witnesses,
let us throw off everything that hinders
and the sin that so easily entangles.
And let us run with perseverance
the race marked out for us,
fixing our eyes on Jesus,
the pioneer and perfecter of faith.
For the joy set before him
he endured the cross,
scorning its shame,
and sat down at the right hand
of the throne of God.

—Hebrews 12:1–2 NIV

6

Amazing Grace

In 1833, the British Parliament honored a man for his Christian leadership in the passage of the 1807 law to abolish the slave trade and the 1833 law to abolish all slavery in the United Kingdom.[77],[78] Parliament resolved to bury this man in Westminster Abbey.

Question: Who was this man who, beginning in the late 1780s, persevered for over forty years to abolish slavery in the United Kingdom?

    a)   William Pitt
    b)   King George III
    c)   William Wilberforce
    d)   John Newton

Some readers may ask, "What does the abolishment of slavery in the United Kingdom have to do with slavery in the United States?"

I invite you to view one of my favorite movies, *Amazing Grace*, and you will find the same evangelical revivals and waves of Great Awakenings that changed the hearts and minds in the United States also brought needed change to the United Kingdom. In fact, the man mentioned above says

---

[77] https://www.westminster-abbey.org/abbey-commemorations/commemorations/william-wilberforce-family.
[78] http://origins.osu.edu/review/after-abolition-britain-and-slave-trade-1807.

his radical reputation to become suddenly a vocal abolitionist is due to his "conversion experience" in 1784–1785.[79]

William Pitt is a good answer but not correct. He was a close friend of the man mentioned above, and they served together in the House of Commons. Pitt eventually became the prime minister, and he supported his friend's numerous resolutions against slavery. Pitt was also given the honor of being buried in Westminster Abbey, next to the man above.[80]

King George III is not the correct answer either. The chapter "The Declaration" delineates why he is an incorrect response.

John Newton is also a great answer but is still not the correct answer. Newton was a former slave trader whose spiritual conversion to Christianity led him to become a devout member of the clergy and an equally devout abolitionist.

This is the same John Newton who in 1779 penned the words to the great Christian hymn "Amazing Grace." I believe this song is about his sin of involvement in the slave trade, his life-changing conversion to Christianity, his repentance and faith in action to abolish slavery, and God's amazing grace and forgiveness. John Newton was a spiritual adviser to William Wilberforce.[81]

---

[79] https://www.britannica.com/biography/William-Wilberforce.
[80] https://www.westminster-abbey.org/abbey-commemorations/commemorations/william-wilberforce-family.
[81] https://www.britannica.com/biography/William-Wilberforce.

Engraved by T.Blood for the European Magazine from an Original Painting by Russell R.A.

William Wilberforce Esq.ʳ M.P.

London - Published by J. Asperne 32 Cornhill 1.ˢᵗ Nov.ʳ 1814.

Wilberforce, William

Answer: The correct answer to the question at the beginning of this *Mercer Moment in American History* is C.

William Wilberforce is buried in Westminster Abbey. His 1784–1785 conversion to evangelical Christianity led him to persevere in the fight to abolish the slave trade and then the abolishment of slavery in the United Kingdom.[82]

Wilberforce was renowned as a devout religious English member of Parliament. He was a close friend of William Pitt, who became the prime minister. Again, John Newton, the author of "Amazing Grace," was a close spiritual adviser.

The lifestyle of William Wilberforce completely changed with his spiritual conversion to evangelical Christianity. His new faith prompted him to be the leading voice in Parliament for social reform, focusing on the abolition of slavery.[83]

Wilberforce entered the House of Commons in 1780. In each session he introduced motions to abolish the slave trade.[84] The powerful economic forces behind slavery clearly targeted Wilberforce. He was quickly branded as a radical.

I believe Wilberforce felt remorse for fellow Christians who said they did not support slavery but were only "stockholders" in certain "shipping companies." That situation reminds me of our present twenty-first century. Some Christians state they do not support abortion but invest in firms that contribute heavily to abortion.

I introduced this chapter with the famous verse from Hebrews on perseverance. For eighteen years, session after session, Wilberforce persevered with bills in Parliament to end the slave trade. He never gave

---

[82] https://www.britannica.com/biography/William-Wilberforce.

[83] http://www.bbc.co.uk/history/historic_figures/wilberforce_william.shtml.

[84] http://www.bbc.co.uk/history/historic_figures/wilberforce_william.shtml.

up. And in 1807, members of Parliament cheered William Wilberforce as the slave trade was finally abolished.[85.]

However, that 1807 law did not change the legal situation for former slaves. William Wilberforce's next goal was the complete emancipation of all slaves. On July 26, 1833, three days before the death of Wilberforce, Parliament passed the Slavery Abolition Act. More than 800,000 slaves in the United Kingdom were set free.[86]

William Wilberforce died on July 29, 1833. The British Parliament declared that Wilberforce should receive the high honor of being interred at Westminster Abbey. He is buried next to his old friend, William Pitt.[87]

---

[85] http://www.bbc.co.uk/history/historic_figures/wilberforce_william.shtml.

[86] https://www.britannica.com/biography/William-Wilberforce.

[87] https://www.britannica.com/biography/William-Wilberforce.

If my people,
who are called by my name,
will humble themselves
and pray and seek my face and turn from their wicked ways,
then I will hear from heaven,
and I will forgive their sin
and will heal their land.

—2 Chronicles 7:14 NIV

7

First Nation to Abolish Slavery

Today, in the twenty-first century, there is much righteous indignation from politicians regarding who to blame for slavery and who should pay any financial reparations to the impacted nations and descendants of slaves. One good starting point might be to study the who, how, and when the world determined to abolish slavery.

Question: Which was the first country (nation, republic, state) to abolish slavery?

   a)   United Kingdom (Britain)
   b)   United States
   c)   A country in Africa
   d)   A country in Asia
   e)   Vermont Republic

One might believe the answer to this *Mercer Moment in American History* will be easy. Surely a country in Africa was the very first in the world to abolish slavery. No.

A second choice might be a country in Asia. No.

My research of eighteenth-century Africa, Asia, and the Middle East found no evidence of a country's rejection of slavery and movement to abolish human slavery. Sadly, for thousands of years prior, slavery was an accepted practice.

There are two nations twenty-first-century politicians criticize the most for slavery. That criticism of the human slave trade is deserved.

However, history documents it was those same two nations that suddenly reversed the course of the world's human slave trade. They led the eighteenth-century world with the powerful weapons of religious and moral indignation to abolish that immoral human slave trade.

Sadly, historians and politicians fail to give the credit due to the Great Awakening of American and British Christians during the 1700s and early 1800s. Religious evangelical revivals fueled an era of deep personal conviction and a call to faith in action for redemption of the sin of slavery.

Politically correct elected officials fail to recognize the historical documentation that the Arab-Muslim slave trade began at least eight hundred years before 1619, when we believe the first African slaves arrived in Jamestown of the Virginia Colony.

Politicians should officially acknowledge that the Arab-Muslim slave trade continued for at least one hundred years after the US Civil War, Lincoln's Emancipation Proclamation, and the passage of Thirteenth Amendment to free all slaves.

I cross-referenced many documents, articles, timelines, and other research to develop this one hundred-year timeline germane to the question.

Key Eighteenth- and Nineteenth-Century Events by Nation, Leading to the Abolishment of Human Slavery

Year	Nation	Event
1888	Brazil	Abolishes slavery.[88]
1886	Cuba	Abolishes slavery.[89]
1865	United States	Thirteenth Amendment abolishes slavery.[90]
1863	Netherlands	Abolishes slavery. [91]
1862	United States	Abraham Lincoln issues his Emancipation Proclamation during the US Civil War; in goes into effect in 1863.[92]
1848	France	Abolishes slavery.[93]
1846	Denmark	Governor proclaims emancipation of slaves in Danish West Indies.[94]
1840	United Kingdom	First World Anti-Slavery Convention meets in London.[95]

[88] https://aaregistry.org/story/brazil-abolishes-slavery/.

[89] https://www.britannica.com/place/Cuba/Sugarcane-and-the-growth-of-slavery.

[90] https://www.history.com/this-day-in-history/house-passes-the-13th-amendment.

[91] https://english.aawsat.com/home/article/2365096/netherlands-marks-anniversary-abolition-slavery.

[92] https://www.history.com/topics/american-civil-war/emancipation-proclamation.

[93] http://slavenorth.com/columns/frenchslavery.htm.

[94] https://www.reuters.com/article/uk-slavery-idUSL1561464920070322.

[95] https://www.historiansagainstslavery.org/main/the-world-antislavery-convention-of-1840/.

Year	Nation	Event
1833	United Kingdom	Passes the Slavery Abolition Act advocated by William Wilberforce. Slave trade was considered piracy, punishable by death. An estimated 800,000 persons freed.[96,97]
1829	Mexico	Abolishes slavery.[98]
1823	United Kingdom	The Anti-Slavery Society is formed. "Christian politician" William Wilberforce, a member of the English Parliament (MEP) was one of the members.[99]
1822	Liberia	Founded by a private group—the American Colonization Society—as a colony in Africa for freed African Americans. Capital city Monrovia was named after US president James Monroe. The population is 85 percent Christian. It declared independence in 1847. [100 101]

---

[96] https://www.reuters.com/article/uk-slavery-idUSL1561464920070322.

[97] https://www.britannica.com/topic/Slavery-Abolition-Act.

[98] https://newstaco.com/2015/02/12/mexicos-black-president-abolished-slavery-before-u-s-civil-war/.

[99] https://www.reuters.com/article/uk-slavery-idUSL1561464920070322.

[100] https://www.history.com/this-day-in-history/liberian-independence-proclaimed.

[101] https://www.blackpast.org/global-african-history/places-global-african-history/monrovia-liberia-1821/.

Year	Nation	Event
1820	United States	US Navy joins Royal Navy to end Atlantic slave trade; antislavery warships deployed to enforce 1808 law to ban slave trade along the coast of West Africa. [102, 103]
1819	United Kingdom	Royal Navy captures slave port and renames it Freetown. It becomes the capital of the first British colony in West Africa, Sierra Leone.[104]
1819	United States	International slave trade declared by Congress to be piracy, punishable by death.[105]

[102] https://military.wikia.org/wiki/West_Africa_Squadron.

[103] https://www.history.navy.mil/content/history/museums/nmusn/explore/exhibits/anti-slave-trade-patrols.html#:~:text=America%20withdrew%20from%20the%20transatlantic%20slave%20trade%20in,off%20West%20Africa%20to%20catch%20American%20slave%20ships.

[104] https://www.forces.net/services/tri-service/how-royal-navy-helped-stop-slave-trade.

[105] https://www.history.navy.mil/research/library/exhibits/anti-slavery-operations-of-the-us-navy.html.

Year	Nation	Event
1808–1860	United Kingdom	Royal Navy places antislavery patrols off the West African coast to enforce the 1809 ban on slave trading. • Zero cooperation from African governments • 3,000-mile coastline • Captures 1,600 slave ships, frees 150,000 Africans • Death rate of British soldiers five times that of other service members. [106, 107, 108]
1813	Sweden	Abolishes slavery.[109]
1811	Spain	Abolishes slavery except in Cuba.[110, 111]

[106] https://www.forces.net/services/tri-service/how-royal-navy-helped-stop-slave-trade.

[107] https://www.history.co.uk/article/the-blockade-of-africa-how-royal-naval-ships-suppressed-the-slave-trade.

[108] http://www.royalnavalmuseum.org/visit_see_victory_cfexhibition_infosheet.html

[109] . https://www.ghanaweb.com/GhanaHomePage/features/The-translantic-slave-trade-A-forgotten-heinous-crime-against-humanity-952177.

[110] https://answers.yahoo.com/question/index?qid=20110131181212AAWEDmo.

[111] https://www.ghanaweb.com/GhanaHomePage/features/The-translantic-slave-trade-A-forgotten-heinous-crime-against-humanity-952177.

Year	Nation	Event
1807	United Kingdom	Passes Abolition of the Slave Trade Act. (*Note:* William Wilberforce filed this legislation in the House of Commons each year for eighteen years until its passage.)[112]
1807	United States	The United States passes legislation banning the slave trade, the importation of new slaves effective from start of 1808.[113]
1806	United States	In a message to Congress, Thomas Jefferson calls for criminalizing the international slave trade (article I, section IX).[114]
1804	United States	All seven Northern states had already abolished slavery.
1787	United States	Founders add article I, section IX of the Constitution, setting 1808 as the year to end the, "Importation of such Persons as any of the States now existing …"[115]

[112] http://abolition.e2bn.org/slavery_113.html.

[113] https://constitutioncenter.org/interactive-constitution/interpretation/article-i/clauses/761.

[114] https://constitutioncenter.org/interactive-constitution/interpretation/article-i/clauses/761.

[115] https://www.usconstitution.net/xconst_A1Sec9.html.

Year	Nation	Event
1785	United States	John Jay, Founding Father and first chief justice of the United States, establishes the New York Manumission Society to promote the abolition of slavery.[116]
1777	Vermont Republic	Constitution of this independent republic outlawed slavery
1772	United Kingdom	"Amazing Grace" is written by former slave trader John Newton. His religious conversion to Christianity made him an abolitionist.[117]
Mid 1700s–late 1800s	United Kingdom, United States	Great Awakening, evangelical Christian religious revivals. Calls to repent for the sin of slavery. Beginning of Antislavery societies and "freedmen" schools.

Answer: The correct answer to this *Mercer Moment in American History* will surprise you: E, Vermont.

This is not meant to be a trick question, just a historical fact.

Few Americans know that in 1777, Vermont was founded as an independent republic with its own constitution. That constitution outlawed slavery in the new 1777 Vermont Republic.

---

[116] https://www.accessible-archives.com/2018/01/abolitionist-john-jay/.
[117] https://www.loc.gov/item/ihas.200149085/.

In the chart above, note that Vermont is not a free state or a slave state. The Vermont Republic is a sovereign and free territory.

In 1791, fourteen years later, Vermont was admitted to the Union as our fourteenth state.

Extra Credit

Question: Which state was an independent nation/republic before it became a state?

- a) Vermont
- b) Texas
- c) Hawaii
- d) California
- e) All the above

Answer: All the above.

Slave Castle – West Africa, Ghana, Cape Coast

Bill of Rights

Congress OF THE United States,

begun and held at the City of, New York, on
Wednesday, the fourth of March, one thousand seven hundred and eighty nine.

The Conventions of a number of the States, having, at the time of their adopting the Constitution, expressed a desire, in order to prevent misconstruction or abuse of its powers, that further declaratory and restrictive clauses should be added: And as extending the ground of public confidence in the Government, will best insure the beneficent ends of its institution:

Resolved, by the SENATE and HOUSE of REPRESENTATIVES of the UNITED STATES of AMERICA in Congress assembled, two thirds of both Houses concurring, That the following Articles be proposed to the Legislatures of the several States, as Amendments to the Constitution of the United States; all, or any of which articles, when ratified by three fourths of the said Legislatures, to be valid to all intents and purposes, as part of the said Constitution, viz.

Articles in addition to, and Amendment of the Constitution of the United States of America, proposed by Congress, and ratified by the Legislatures of the several States, pursuant to the fifth Article of the Original Constitution.

Article the first ...... After the first enumeration required by the first Article of the Constitution, there shall be one Representative for every thirty thousand, until the number shall amount to one hundred, after which, the proportion shall be so regulated by Congress, that there shall be not less than one hundred Representatives, nor less than one Representative for every forty thousand persons, until the number of Representatives shall amount to two hundred, after which, the proportion shall be so regulated by Congress, that there shall not be less than two hundred Representatives, nor more than one Representative for every fifty thousand persons.   [Not Ratified]

Article the second .... No law, varying the compensation for the services of the Senators and Representatives, shall take effect, until an election of Representatives shall have intervened.   [Not Ratified]

Article the third .... Congress shall make no law respecting an establishment of religion, or prohibiting the free exercise thereof; or abridging the freedom of speech, or of the press; or the right of the people peaceably to assemble, and to petition the Government for a redress of grievances.

Article the fourth ..... A well regulated Militia, being necessary to the security of a free State, the right of the people to keep and bear Arms, shall not be infringed.

Article the fifth .... No Soldier shall, in time of peace, be quartered in any house, without the consent of the owner, nor in time of war, but in a manner to be prescribed by law.

Article the sixth ...... The right of the people to be secure in their persons, houses, papers, and effects, against unreasonable searches and seizures, shall not be violated, and no Warrants shall issue but upon probable cause, supported by oath or affirmation, and particularly describing the place to be searched, and the persons or things to be seized.

Article the seventh ... No person shall be held to answer for a capital, or otherwise infamous crime, unless on a presentment or indictment of a grand jury, except in cases arising in the land or Naval forces, or in the Militia, when in actual service in time of War or public danger; nor shall any person be subject for the same offence to be twice put in jeopardy of life or limb; nor shall be compelled in any criminal case, to be a witness against himself, nor be deprived of life, liberty, or property, without due process of law; nor shall private property be taken for public use without just compensation.

Article the eighth ..... In all criminal prosecutions, the accused shall enjoy the right to a speedy and public trial by an impartial jury of the State and district wherein the crime shall have been committed, which district shall have been previously ascertained by law, and to be informed of the nature and cause of the accusation; to be confronted with the witnesses against him; to have compulsory process for obtaining witnesses in his favor, and to have the assistance of counsel for his defence.

Article the ninth ...... In suits at common law, where the value in controversy shall exceed twenty dollars, the right of trial by jury shall be preserved, and no fact, tried by a jury, shall be otherwise re-examined in any Court of the United States, than according to the rules of the common law.

Article the tenth .... Excessive bail shall not be required, nor excessive fines imposed, nor cruel and unusual punishments inflicted.

Article the eleventh .. The enumeration in the Constitution, of certain rights, shall not be construed to deny or disparage others retained by the people.

Article the twelfth .... The powers not delegated to the United States by the Constitution, nor prohibited by it to the States, are reserved to the States respectively, or to the people.

Frederick Augustus Muhlenberg Speaker of the House of Representatives.

John Adams, Vice President of the United States, and President of the Senate.

ATTEST,

John Beckley, Clerk of the House of Representatives.

Sam. A. Otis Secretary of the Senate.

8

The Gag Rule

A "gag rule" is a parliamentary procedure used by members of decision-making bodies, where they agree to limit or "table" the raising, consideration, or discussion of a controversial topic.

The most famous gag rule began with the 1836 Congress's attempt to prevent the discussion and debate of slavery.[118]

Question: Who was the main target of the 1836–1844 series of gag rules in the House of Representatives?

a) John Quincy Adams
b) President Andrew Jackson
c) Rep. Henry Pinckney, South Carolina
d) John Hammond, South Carolina

Imagine you are elected by your constituents to serve on your local school board or city council.

Imagine your other elected colleagues know there is one issue of yours they wish to avoid. Your fellow members vote to "gag" you, meaning that your item will never be allowed for consideration or discussion. There will never be a vote on your issue.

---

[118] https://www.britannica.com/topic/gag-rule.

Now imagine that you are not just any member of that elected body. You were once the president of the United States of America.

The First Amendment of our Constitution includes the right to "petition the Government for a redress of grievances."[119] In fact, the thought process is often coupled as the "right of the people peaceably to assemble" with the result being "to petition the Government for a redress of grievances."[120]

Our First Amendment right of petition, though not a source of conflict and debate in the twenty-first century, became a huge national focus in the early 1830s. Citizens filed petitions to Congress asking for consideration and debate on the abolishment of slavery.

How did Congress respond?

On May 26, 1836, Congressman Henry Pinckney of South Carolina led the so-called Jacksonian Democrats in the passage of the following gag rule to forbid the consideration of antislavery petitions:

> Resolved, That all petitions, memorials, resolutions, propositions, or papers, relating in any way or to any extent whatever to the subject of slavery, or the abolition of slavery, shall, without being either printed or referred, be laid upon the table, and that no further action whatever shall be had thereon.[121]

---

[119] https://constitution.congress.gov/constitution/amendment-1/.

[120] https://constitution.congress.gov/constitution/amendment-1/.

[121] https://www.blackpast.org/african-american-history/1836-gag-rule-pinckney-resolution-3/.

*John Quincy Adams (1767 - 1848) - American statesman and
the sixth president of the United States from 1825 to 1829.*

To table is a parliamentary procedure that effectively kills an item.

A representative from Massachusetts raised the first objection to the new gag rule. Records state that Congressman John Quincy Adams shouted during the roll-call vote:

> I hold the resolution to be a direct violation of the Constitution of the United States.[122]

Please note this 1836 gag rule was a resolution and not a standing rule of the House of Representatives. As such, it had to be passed each session of the House.

However, the US Archives document that on January 8, 1840, after receiving more than 130,000 citizen petitions to abolish slavery, the House then adopted this standing rule:

> That no petition, memorial, resolution, or other paper praying the abolition of slavery in the District of Columbia, or any State or Territories of the United States in which it now exists, shall be received by this House, or entertained in any way whatever.[123], [124]

Note the key addition in the 1840 gag rule. Not only would antislavery petitions never be put to debate, the House would now refuse even to receive those citizen petitions!

The key target of the gag rule was again Representative John Quincy Adams, the former president.

---

[122] https://www.visitthecapitol.gov/exhibitions/artifact/representative-john-quincy-adamss-motion-denouncing-gag-rule-unconstitutional.

[123] https://constitutingamerica.org/freedom-of-speech-within-congressional-debates-john-quincy-adams-the-gag-rule-1840s/.

[124] https://law.jrank.org/pages/7061/Gag-Rule.html.

Answer: The correct answer to the question at the beginning of this *Mercer Moment in American History* is A.

Again, the central objective of the 1836–1844 gag rule was to silence Representative John Quincy Adams. He was a former US president who lost his bid for reelection to Andrew Jackson, a slaveowner Democrats point to as the founder of their Democratic Party.

John Quincy Adams was the first and only American president to serve later in Congress.

For eight years the Jacksonian Democrats were successful in gagging any attempt by Adams to bring the, "citizen's petition for the abolishment of slavery" up for discussion, debate, and a vote.

In 1844, Representative John Quincy Adams wrote a congressional resolution to repeal the gag rule. He expertly created a coalition to support and help pass his resolution.

Finally, after eight years of gagging a former president, on December 3, 1844, the gag rule was repealed by a vote of 108–80.

Trans-Atlantic Slave Trade	
Brazil	4.5 to 5.0 Million
Central America	200K
East Coast of South America	500K
Europe	200K to 300K
Guianas	500K
West Indies	4.5 to 5.0 Million
United States	380K-500K

Historical records document approximately 12 million humans were captured by slave raiders in Africa, sold, and then transported to the Americas.

Of the 11 million slaves who survived the voyage, sources estimate 380,0000 to 500,000 arrived in what is now known as the United States.

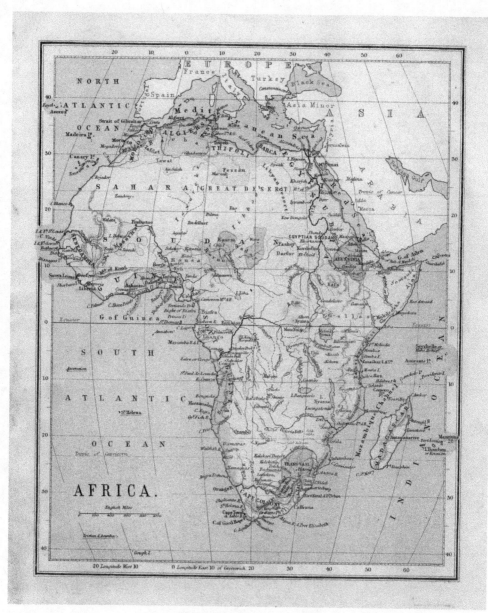

Mid-Victorian map of Africa

9

Percentage of Slaves Transported to the United States

The transatlantic slave trade documented the purchase of 12.5 million Africans from their captors, the dominant and powerful African and Arab-Muslim tribes.[125]

It is estimated 10.7 million of these new slaves survived the trip from Africa across the Atlantic Ocean to the "New World" of North America, the Caribbean, and South America.

Question: What percentage of those 10.7 million African slaves were transported to the thirteen colonies of what became the United States?

a. 75 percent
b. 5 percent or less
c. 25 percent
d. 50 percent

Let us be clear: Slavery is what I term as EDS—evil, demonic, and satanic. Those who captured, bought, sold, or transported human slaves are all equally guilty.

---

[125] http://slaveryandremembrance.org/articles/article/?id=A0002.

Whether a nation negotiated for one slave or ten million slaves, the business of human slavery was again evil, demonic, and satanic.

The agenda taught today by many colleges and universities is that slavery is unique to the United States and seemingly a sin linked only to Western civilization. Too many students believe that the blame for the transatlantic slave trade lies solely with White Europeans, who kidnapped and sold slaves from the continent of Africa. Colleges and universities who are in the conversation and debate about reparations for the descendants of slaves wrongly focus their rebuke solely on the United States.

The capture of African slaves in the acclaimed movies *Roots* and *Amistad* has led to confusion among many of the intellectual elite. In fact, Dr. Henry Louis Gates Jr. of Harvard stated the following in his 2010 op-ed in the *Dallas Morning News*:

> Advocates of reparations for the descendants of those slaves generally ignore this untidy problem of the significant role that Africans played in the trade.
>
> Historians John Thornton and Linda Heywood of Boston University estimate 90 percent of those shipped to the New World were enslaved by Africans and then sold to European traders.[126]

In the summer of 2020, I began reviewing the works of Dr John Alembellah Azumah of Gambia, particularly his book *The Legacy of Arab-Islam in Africa*. Dr. Azumah is a scholar and researcher with impressive credentials. He earned a PhD from the University of Birmingham, England; and his résumé includes serving as the director for the Centre of Islamic Studies at the London School of Theology, and as professor of world Christianity and Islam at Columbia Theological Seminary.[127]

---

[126] https://www.dallasnews.com/opinion/commentary/2010/05/01/henry-louis-gates-jr-africans-role-in-the-slave-trade/.

[127] https://berkleycenter.georgetown.edu/people/john-azumah.

Dr. Azumah complains that Western slavery is demonized, which it should be. However, the Arab-Muslim slavery of the so-called Golden Age is romanticized, which it should not be. He describes in detail a systematic and religious capturing and selling of fellow Africans into slavery. (Later in my book I share more research gathered from Dr. Azumah and other African scholars.)

Dr. Azumah states that only 5 percent of the African victims of the transatlantic slave trade went to America's thirteen colonies. The other 95 percent were sent to the Caribbean and South America.

> It is estimated that possibly as many as 11 million Africans were transported across the Atlantic, 95% of which went to South and Central America, mainly to Portuguese, Spanish and French possessions; only 5% of the slaves ended up in what we call the United States today.[128]

Dr. Azumah also documents his belief that the mortality rate for slaves crossing the Atlantic was much lower than for those who were shipped to other parts of the world.

> While the mortality rate of the slaves being transported across the Atlantic was as high as 10%, the percentage of the slaves dying in transit in the Tran-Saharan and East African slave market was a staggering 80 to 90%.[129]

The transatlantic slave trade database documents over 36,000 voyages between 1525 and 1866. The database points to 10.7 million slaves taken from sub-Saharan Africa who survived the crossing of the Atlantic. This means that about 4 to five percent of the slaves were transported to America's thirteen colonies. "Only about 388,000 were transported directly from Africa to North America."[130]

---

[128] https://adarapress.com/2016/09/14/comparing-the-islamic-slave-to-the-american-slave-trade-the-legacy-of-arab-islam-in-africa-dr-john-azumah-video/.

[129] https://adarapress.com/2016/09/14/comparing-the-islamic-slave-to-the-american-slave-trade-the-legacy-of-arab-islam-in-africa-dr-john-azumah-video/.

[130] https://www.slavevoyages.org/assessment/estimates.

Trans-Atlantic Imports by Region [131] 1450-1900		
Region	**Number of slaves accounted for**	**%**
Brazil	4, 000, 000	35.4
Spanish Empire	2, 500, 000	22.1
British West Indies	2, 000, 000	17.7
French West Indies	1, 600, 000	14.1
British North America and United States	500, 000	4.4
Dutch West Indies	500, 000	4.4
Danish West Indies	28, 000	0.2
Europe (and Islands)	200, 000	1.8
Total	**11, 328, 000**	**100**

Again, whether 4 percent or 5 percent, today we all agree that the transatlantic slave trade was evil and wrong. But why should the subject of reparation payments always seem limited to North America?

Another point of issue: Does the human slave trade still exist in twenty-first-century Africa?

_____

_____

Answer: The correct answer to the question at the beginning of this *Mercer Moment in American History* is B.

Five percent or less, about 400,000 of the 10.7 million slaves that arrived in the New World, were transported to what is now the United States.[132]

---

[131] https://i.pinimg.com/originals/ef/c1/4c/efc14cd73794a4b448bcd2f4abe 56982.jpg

[132] https://www.slavevoyages.org/assessment/estimates.

I end this chapter with two extremely interesting, albeit controversial perspectives from African American economist Thomas Sowell. He is a graduate of Harvard with a doctorate from the University of Chicago. Dr. Sowell is currently a senior fellow at Stanford University's Hoover Institution.[133] I challenge readers to perform your own analysis of Dr. Sowell's work and the review data that forms his perspective.

Regarding the overwhelming roles and responsibility of the Arab-Muslim slavers, Sowell writes,

> More whites were brought as slaves to North Africa than blacks brought as slaves to the United States or to the 13 colonies from which it was formed.

> White slaves were still being bought and sold in the Ottoman Empire, decades after blacks were freed in the United States.[134], [135]

And finally, Sowell states the following about the twelve centuries of Arab-Muslim slavers and white slavery:

> Of all the tragic facts about the history of slavery, the most astonishing to an American today is that, although slavery was a worldwide institution for thousands of years, nowhere in the world was slavery a controversial issue prior to the 18th century.

> People of every race and color were enslaved—and enslaved others. White people were still being bought and sold as slaves in the Ottoman Empire, decades after American blacks were freed.[136]

---

[133] http://www.tsowell.com/.

[134] https://skeptics.stackexchange.com/questions/47867/were-more-whites-slaves-brought-to-north-africa-than-black-slaves-were-brought-t.

[135] https://www.hannenabintuherland.com/usa/larry-elder-more-whites-brought-as-slaves-to-north-africa-than-blacks-to-us-herland-report/.

[136] https://www.right-mind.us/thomas-sowell-on-slavery-and-this-fact-there-are-more-slaves-today-than-were-seized-from-africa-in-four-centuries/.

DRED SCOTT.

10

1857 Dred Scott Decision

In the famous 1857 Dred Scott decision, the Southern-influenced Supreme Court ruled that African Americans, whether free or enslaved, were not citizens and that the Missouri Compromise, which was meant to balance the admittance of free and slave states, was unconstitutional.[137]

The 1857 Supreme Court Dred Scott decision was overturned by which constitutional amendment(s)?

a) Thirteenth Amendment
b) Fourteenth Amendment
c) Fifteenth Amendment
d) Thirteenth and Fourteenth Amendments
e) None of the above; the Dred Scott decision was never overturned.

In 1857, the US Supreme Court decided the landmark *Dred Scott v. Sandford* case by a 7–2 vote. The majority opinion was authored and delivered by Chief Justice Roger B. Taney, a Jacksonian Democrat and former slave owner.[138] The critical dissent of two justices in the minority was written by John McLean of Ohio and Benjamin R. Curtis of Massachusetts.

Dred Scott was an African American slave. He was considered the property of the Peter Blow family in Missouri, a slave state. Scott was sold to US

---

137 https://www.britannica.com/event/Dred-Scott-decision.
138 https://www.britannica.com/event/Dred-Scott-decision.

Army Surgeon John Emerson of Missouri, who took him to Illinois, a free state, and later to the Wisconsin territory, a free territory.[139]

Emerson returned with Scott to Missouri and died in 1847. Scott later sued in state courts for his freedom. He believed the journeys to a state and then a territory where slavery was prohibited made him a free man. There was a "Once free, always free" doctrine often upheld by Missouri courts in determining slave freedom suits.[140]

Scott lost in the state courts and eventually ended up in the possession of John Stanford of New York. Dred Scott sued in federal courts, and the case rose to the Supreme Court.

Chief Justice Roger B. Taney authored and read the majority opinion stating that African Americans, free or slaves, were not citizens of the United States and, therefore, could not legally sue.[141]

Then Taney went further. he struck down the Missouri Compromise as unconstitutional and wrote that Congress had no authority to ban slavery in any federal territory. Taney also determined that the Fifth Amendment of the Constitution protected slaveowners from being deprived of their "property."[142, 143]

I am not an attorney, but I wonder how many constitutional scholars would agree with me that this majority opinion of the Supreme Court may be the worst ever written. Is there any other Supreme Court decision that caused more division among the legal community?

Some believed the Supreme Court's Dred Scott decision was meant to prevent a civil war. Wrong. The majority 7–2 opinion of this case provoked the Civil War.

---

[139] https://www.britannica.com/event/Dred-Scott-decision.

[140] https://www.history.com/topics/black-history/dred-scott-case.

[141] https://www.history.com/topics/black-history/dred-scott-case.

[142] https://www.history.com/topics/black-history/dred-scott-case.

[143] https://supreme.justia.com/cases/federal/us/60/393/.

Life and Portrait of Fugitive Slave Anthony Burns, whose arrest and trial under the Fugitive Slave Act of 1850 fueled riots and protests by abolitionists and citizens of Boston in the spring of 1854.

Justices McLean and Curtis argued in devastating dissents that even at our nation's founding, several states considered African Americans to be citizens and that they even had the privilege to vote.[144] Justice Curtis wrote,

> All free native-born inhabitants of the States of New Hampshire, Massachusetts, New York, New Jersey, and North Carolina, though descended from African slaves, were not only citizens of those States, but such of them as had the other necessary qualifications possessed the franchise of electors, on equal terms with other citizens.[145]

Justice Curtis argued they could not be denied the right to claim citizenship.

The US Congress and antislavery states would require constitutional amendments to override this 1857 Supreme Court decision and eventually abolish slavery and establish citizenship.

Answer: The correct and best answer to this *Mercer Moment in American History* is D, the Thirteenth and Fourteenth Amendments.

While some might argue only the 14th Amendment, I passionately believe the best answer is the Thirteenth and Fourteenth Amendments.[146],[147] The Thirteenth Amendment to the US Constitution abolished slavery and involuntary servitude. The Fourteenth Amendment granted citizenship to all persons born or naturalized in the United States, including former slaves.

Again, the Thirteenth and Fourteenth Amendments together overrode the majority opinion of Chief Justice Roger B. Taney regarding the 1857 Dred Scott decision.

---

[144] http://totallyhistory.com/dred-scott-v-sandford/.

[145] https://supreme.justia.com/cases/federal/us/60/393/.

[146] http://totallyhistory.com/dred-scott-v-sandford/.

[147] https://supreme.justia.com/cases/federal/us/60/393/.

JOHN BROWN

HARRIET B. STOWE

WM. L. GARRISON

CHARLES SUMNER

HORACE GREELEY

WM. WILBERFORCE

THE ABOLITION MOVEMENT.

Historical Irony

Question: Who was the chief justice of the United States who swore in President Abraham Lincoln?

Answer: Chief Justice Roger B. Taney.

Yes, the same Justice Taney who authored the majority opinion of the 1857 Dred Scott decision.[148]

---

[148] https://www.history.com/topics/black-history/dred-scott-case.

Then I heard the voice of the Lord saying,
"Whom shall I send?
And who will go for us?"
And I said,
"Here am I. Send me!"

—Isaiah 6:8 NIV

11

Republican Slaves?

The 1860 Census determined the population of the United States to be 31.4 million persons. This included 3.95 million slaves.[149]

Question: In 1860, what percentage of slaves were owned by Republicans?

  a) 42 percent
  b) 31 percent
  c) 19.3 percent
  d) Far fewer than 1 percent

[149] https://www.census.gov/library/publications/1864/dec/1860a.html

Historians believe the Republican Party began in the 1850s in response to the passage of the Kansas-Nebraska Act, which was sponsored by Democratic senator Stephen A. Douglas.

In 1820, the Missouri Compromise passed, which admitted Missouri as a slave state and Maine as a free state. This hotly debated compromise was agreed on to try to preserve the critical and delicate balance of power in Congress between free states and slave states.

However, with the passage of Senator Douglas's Kansas-Nebraska Act, American territories that became new states could now, under "popular sovereignty," all decide to become future slave states. Interestingly enough, this is the same Douglas of the famous Lincoln-Douglas debates.[150], [151]

As you may imagine, Northern abolitionists were incensed. In March 1854, political antislavery leaders and groups opposed to this expansion of slavery held meetings in Ripon, Wisconsin. This is considered the birth or founding of the new Republican Party. The first convention of this new political party was held a few months later, in July 1854 in Jackson, Michigan.[152], [153]

Over the next six years, the membership of the new Republican Party grew with Northern abolitionists, white protestants, and African Americans.

In 1860, the pivotal Republican convention had 466 delegates, who nominated Abraham Lincoln of Illinois as their candidate for president. Following are a few key excerpts from the platform adopted by that 1860 Republican convention.[154]

---

[150] https://www.history.com/this-day-in-history/republican-party-founded.
[151] https://www.britannica.com/topic/Republican-Party.
[152] https://www.history.com/this-day-in-history/republican-party-founded.
[153] https://www.britannica.com/topic/Republican-Party.
[154] https://www.historytoday.com/archive/republican-party-founded.

1860 Republican Party Platform

That the maintenance of the principles promulgated in the Declaration of Independence and embodied in the Federal Constitution,

"That all men are created equal; that they are endowed by their Creator with certain inalienable rights; that among these are life, liberty and the pursuit of happiness; that to secure these rights, governments are instituted among men, deriving their just powers from the consent of the governed,"

is essential to the preservation of our Republican institutions; and that the Federal Constitution, the Rights of the States, and the Union of the States must and shall be preserved.

...

That the normal condition of all the territory of the United States is that of freedom: That, as our Republican fathers, when they had abolished slavery in all our national territory, ordained that "no persons should be deprived of life, liberty or property without due process of law,"

it becomes our duty, by legislation, whenever such legislation is necessary, to maintain this provision of the Constitution against all attempts to violate it;

and we deny the authority of Congress, of a territorial legislature, or of any individuals, to give legal existence to slavery in any territory of the United States.

That we brand the recent reopening of the African slave trade, under the cover of our national flag, aided by perversions of judicial power, as a crime against humanity and a burning shame to our country and age;

and we call upon Congress to take prompt and efficient measures for the total and final suppression of that execrable traffic.[155]

---

[155] https://www.presidency.ucsb.edu/documents/republican-party-platform-1860.

In that 1860 election 1,866,452 Americans cast their vote for Lincoln and the "antislavery" Republican Party.[156]

Before Lincoln was inaugurated in March 1861, seven Southern slave states seceded, beginning with South Carolina in December 1860. Those seven states formed the Confederate States of America.[157]

Given the above scenario and agenda of the new Republican Party, the seemingly easy answer to the question of how many Republicans owned slaves in 1860 should be 0 percent.

However, liberal historians argue that as many as eight or more of those first Republicans may have once owned slaves. Their frequent target is Republican president Ulysses S. Grant.

I need to give a hat tip to my friend Dinesh D'Souza for pointing me in the right direction for my research. The accurate history of Grant is the best example to combat the agenda of today's historical revisionists.

Ulysses S. Grant was the son of Jesse Grant, a vocal abolitionist from Illinois. After graduating from West Point and serving a few years in the military, he married Julia Dent, whose father was a slave owner from Missouri.[158],[159],[160] Upset at Ulysses marrying into a slave-owning family, no one from the abolitionist Grant family attended the wedding.[161]

In 1858, Julia's father gave them a thirty-five-year-old man named William Jones.[162] Grant's neighbors made fun of Ulysses as they witnessed him

---

[156] https://www.history.com/this-day-in-history/republican-party-founded.

[157] https://www.history.com/this-day-in-history/republican-party-founded.

[158] https://www.britannica.com/biography/Ulysses-S-Grant.

[159] https://www.history.com/topics/us-presidents/ulysses-s-grant-1.

[160] https://www.worldatlas.com/articles/at-the-start-of-the-american-civil-war-u-s-grant-held-slaves-robert-e-lee-did-not.html.

[161] https://civilwartalk.com/threads/ulysses-s-grant-touted-as-one-of-the-great-civil-rights-presidents.145342/.

[162] https://www.nationalreview.com/2020/06/in-defense-of-ulysses-s-grant/.

working side by side with Jones in the fields.[163] In fact, one document has a neighbor stating this about Grant: "He is not a slavery man."[164]

One year later Grant, even though he was in poverty and needed the money, freed William Jones. He may have been offered as much as $1,000 ($30,000 in today's money) for Jones.[165] But Grant refused to sell him and instead wrote, "I do hereby manumit, emancipate and set free said William Jones from slavery forever."[166]

---

[163] https://www.nationalreview.com/2020/06/in-defense-of-ulysses-s-grant/.

[164] https://www.worldatlas.com/articles/at-the-start-of-the-american-civil-war-u-s-grant-held-slaves-robert-e-lee-did-not.html.

[165] https://civilwartalk.com/threads/ulysses-s-grant-touted-as-one-of-the-great-civil-rights-presidents.145342/.

[166] https://www.worldatlas.com/articles/at-the-start-of-the-american-civil-war-u-s-grant-held-slaves-robert-e-lee-did-not.html.

General Ulysses S. Grant. He graduated from West Point in 1843 and served valiantly during the Mexican-American War under Winfield Scott and future president Zachary Taylor. Between wars Grant struggled at several occupations before rejoining the Army after Confederate forces fired upon Fort Sumter. Championed by President Lincoln as an aggressive fighter, Grant was named general-in-chief of the Army and after the war became the 18th President of the United States.

In August 1859, Grant applied for a position of importance and influence as a county engineer. On paper, his West Point education, military experience, and references made him extremely well-qualified.[167] However, the Republican commissioners deciding who to hire were concerned because Grant's father-in-law was a slave-owning Democrat.[168] Any tiebreaker was lost when Grant, ever honest, shared that because of his personal dislike for the Republican candidate in the 1856 presidential election, he voted for Democrat James Buchanan.[169]

So yes, some could say Ulysses S. Grant owned one slave in 1858. But at that time, Ulysses S. Grant was voting Democrat, not Republican.[170]

All that changed quickly when Ulysses S. Grant witnessed firsthand the horrors of slavery. He led the Union forces as the commanding general of the US Army, defeated the South to win the Civil War, and in 1869, became the Republican president during Reconstruction.

Honestly, I believe the correct answer to the question at the beginning of this *Mercer Moment in American History* is actually 0 percent as in 1860, no Republicans owned slaves.

_____

_____

Answer: However, given the Grant example used by the political agenda of some, the "safe" or "best" answer is D.

Again, to avoid dispute from political and historical revisionists, in 1860 far fewer than 1 percent of the 3.9 million slaves were owned by Republicans.

---

[167] https://www.biography.com/us-president/ulysses-s-grant.
[168] https://www.nationalreview.com/2020/06/in-defense-of-ulysses-s-grant/.
[169] https://en.wikipedia.org/wiki/Ulysses_S._Grant#CITEREFMcFeely1981.
[170] https://www.factcheck.org/2007/12/presidents-who-owned-slaves/.

Extra Credit

Question: Who was the last US president to own slaves while in office?

a) Democrat John Tyler, the tenth president
b) Democrat James K. Polk, the eleventh president.
c) Democrat Zachary Taylor, the twelfth president.
d) Democrat Andrew Johnson, the seventeenth president
e) Republican Ulysses S. Grant, the eighteenth president

Answer: The correct answer is C, Democrat Zachary Taylor, the twelfth president.

Zachary Taylor served as president only sixteen months, from 1849–1850. He died suddenly of a stomach disease on July 9, 1850. Taylor owned slaves, perhaps as many as 150, during his brief time as president.[171]

Extra Credit

In the 2020 presidential election the Democratic nominee, Joe Biden, stated that Republican president Donald J. Trump was the first "racist" president. Considering the history of the Democratic Party and slavery, this was a profound accusation.

Question: Andrew Jackson is considered the founder of the Democratic Party. Since Andrew Jackson, which president, if any owned slaves while in office?

Answer:

President	Year	Party	Number of Slaves while President
John Tyler	1841–1845	Whig/Democrat	70
James K. Polk	1845–1849	Democrat	25
Zachary Taylor	1849–1850	Democrat/Whig	150

---

[171] https://www.factcheck.org/2007/12/presidents-who-owned-slaves/.

Then the Lord said to Moses,
"Go to Pharaoh and say to him,
'This is what the Lord,
the God of the Hebrews, says:
"Let my people go,
so that they may worship me."'

—Exodus 9:1 NIV

— 12 —

Moses of the Underground Railroad

Moses is known as the great leader, lawgiver, and prophet who led the Hebrew people from slavery in Egypt to freedom in the Promised Land.

The Underground Railroad also had a "Moses" who led African American slaves to freedom.

Question: Which person listed below was known as the "Moses" of the Underground Railroad?

a) Frederick Douglass
b) Crispus Attucks
c) Wentworth Cheswell
d) Harriett Tubman

Monument to the Underground Railroad

The Underground Railroad was not a physical railroad. In the mid-nineteenth century, it was a huge network in the United States made up of secret routes, secret persons, and secret hideouts established before the Civil War. The Underground Railroad was created, funded, and managed by white Christian abolitionists, free Northern African Americans, and former slaves to help fugitive slaves from the South escape to freedom in Northern United States and Canada. It is estimated that before the Civil War, the Underground Railroad helped over 100,000 African American slaves from the South escape and find freedom.

To readers, especially students, each of these names listed deserves your consideration for future essays and diligent study. However, only one was nicknamed "Moses."

Frederick Douglass was a former slave who escaped, taught himself to read, and became an ordained minister of the African Methodist Episcopal (AME) Zion Church.[172]

A gifted orator, Douglass was a prominent national leader and activist in the movement to abolish slavery.[173] Douglass became a key counselor to President Abraham Lincoln. He promoted the emancipation of slaves and future voting rights.[174], [175]

Frederick Douglass was a leader in the recruiting of former slaves to serve in the Union Army, including two of his sons who served. He strongly advocated for providing uniforms and the arming of the African American soldiers for the army.[176]

Crispus Attucks, I am proud to say, was added to our US history standards for the state of Texas. I teamed with my colleague, David Bradley of Beaumont, Texas, to ensure Attucks was included in the curriculum.

---

[172] https://www.history.com/topics/black-history/frederick-douglass.
[173] https://www.history.com/topics/black-history/frederick-douglass.
[174] https://www.history.com/topics/black-history/frederick-douglass.
[175] http://www.pbs.org/thisfarbyfaith/people/frederick_douglass.html.
[176] https://www.britannica.com/biography/Frederick-Douglass.

Crispus Attucks was the first American killed in the Boston Massacre. That means he was the first martyr of the American Revolution.[177]

Wentworth Cheswell is considered the first African American elected to office in the United States. In 1768, as a twenty-two-year-old, he was elected in Newmarket, New Hampshire, as town constable. Later in life, Cheswell held several other offices, including auditor, justice of the peace, and town messenger of the committee on safety.[178]

The New England Historical Society states that Wentworth Cheswell was one of the men who rode with Paul Revere on that famous "midnight ride" to "warn Portsmouth citizens of the approach of two British warships."[179]

Answer: The correct answer to the *Mercer Moment in American History* is D, Harriett Tubman.

In the early 1820s, Harriet Tubman was born on a slave plantation in Maryland with the name Araminta "Minty" Ross. In 1844, she married John Tubman, a free black man. That marriage did not end well.[180]

In 1849, Tubman escaped from the slave plantation in Maryland. With the help of the Underground Railroad, Tubman walked only at night over ninety miles to find her freedom in Philadelphia.[181], [182]

---

[177] https://www.history.com/news/crispus-attucks-american-revolution-boston-massacre.

[178] https://www.newenglandhistoricalsociety.com/wentworth-cheswell-black-man-rode-paul-revere/.

[179] https://www.newenglandhistoricalsociety.com/wentworth-cheswell-black-man-rode-paul-revere/.

[180] https://www.history.com/topics/black-history/harriet-tubman.

[181] https://www.history.com/topics/black-history/harriet-tubman.

[182] https://www.biography.com/activist/harriet-tubman.

Harriet Tubman was an abolitionist and political activist.
Born into slavery, Tubman escaped and led many missions
to rescue slaves using the network of anti-slavery activists
and safe houses known as the Underground Railroad."

It is not clear when she changed her name to Harriett.

Tubman created her own network for the Underground Railroad and bravely went back several times to the slave plantations of the South to free loved ones and friends.

Harriet Tubman is by far the most famous "conductor" of the Underground Railroad. Historians differ on the number, but Tubman led between thirteen and nineteen "rescue missions" that freed between seventy and three hundred slaves.[183], [184]

Historians do agree that not one slave under Tubman's care was ever caught or executed. All former slaves made it to freedom. Every researcher remarks on Tubman's strong Christian faith and that she was a gun-toting African American female conductor of the Underground Railroad.

The fame of Harriet Tubman brought tremendous risks, which were amplified by the passage of the 1850 Fugitive Slave Act. If she had been captured, it would have meant the penalty of death.[185]

During the Civil War, Harriet Tubman knew a Union victory meant freedom for all slaves. She worked for the Union Army as a nurse, a scout, and even as a Union spy.[186]

Some historians point to Harriet Tubman as the first woman to lead an armed raid in a war. She helped guide a military expedition and subsequent raids of several Southern plantations along the Combahee River, freeing over seven hundred slaves.[187]

It is clear to understand why Harriet Tubman is affectionately known as the "Moses of her people."

---

[183] https://www.history.com/topics/black-history/harriet-tubman.

[184] https://www.biography.com/activist/harriet-tubman.

[185] https://www.biography.com/activist/harriet-tubman.

[186] https://www.biography.com/activist/harriet-tubman.

[187] https://www.biography.com/activist/harriet-tubman

Mercer Moment in Political Irony

Who will replace Andrew Jackson on the new twenty dollar bill?

Answer: Abolitionist Harriet Tubman, the "Moses of her people," will replace Andrew Jackson, the founder of the Democratic Party and a slave owner.

Have I not commanded you?
Be strong and courageous.
Do not be afraid;
do not be discouraged,
for the Lord your God will be with you
wherever you go.

—Joshua 1:9 NIV

13

First African American Medal of Honor Recipient

The Medal of Honor is the highest military award presented by the United States to a member of the armed forces. Recipients distinguished themselves by risking their own lives above and beyond the call of duty in action against an enemy of the United States.

Question: Who was the first African American recipient of the Medal of Honor?

a) First Sergeant Alexander Kelly
b) Corporal Decatur Dorsey
c) Private Charles Veal
d) Sergeant William Carney

As I researched this question and chapter, I found that we are all witnesses to the results of the teaching by too many university professors regarding the flag of the United States of America. Their lectures advance their biases of our flag as a symbol of racism and hate.

May God help those honest students who believe in academic freedom and who would dare to raise a hand in class to question a professor's personal bias impacting his or her instruction.

The four gentlemen listed above would each question those same professors. These four men are all Civil War heroes who, during that war, were four out of a total of twenty-five African American recipients of the Medal of Honor.[188]

Please notice what I just documented—twenty-five African Americans were recipients of our nation's highest honor for their actions during the 1860s. Each of these men distinguished himself by risking his life to raise and carry the flag or "colors" after a fellow soldier and flag bearer was mortally wounded. In fact, my study found at least eight of those twenty-five African American recipients were each recognized in battle for their bravery in seizing the Union flag to lead and rally their fellow soldiers.[189]

Note in my final comments that each of these men is from a different army company and different division, all performing their acts of bravery in a different Civil War battle.

So why was that Union flag so special and important?

The 1863 Emancipation Proclamation of Abraham Lincoln freed slaves in the Confederate States and allowed the men the choice to enlist in the army. Guess which army and which flag these new 180,000 African American soldiers chose to serve?

Movies such as *Glory* and *The Patriot* remind us of the importance of the American flag. Soldiers would throw down their weapons to raise, wave, and carry our flag after a fellow soldier had fallen. In a fierce battle, the raised flag meant there were those still in the battle. And with all the chaos and confusion, our soldiers looked for our flag as a rallying point to come and stand together.

---

[188] Congressional Medal of Honor Society, https://www.cmohs.org/news-events/blog/honoring-the-african-american-recipients-of-the-civil-war/.
[189] Congressional Medal of Honor Society, https://www.cmohs.org/news-events/blog/honoring-the-african-american-recipients-of-the-civil-war/.

The 54th Regiment Massachusetts Volunteer Infantry at Fort Wagner, South Carolina. Authorized by the Emancipation Proclamation, this regiment consisted of African-American enlisted men commanded by white officers.

Unfortunately, the man carrying that flag was a key target of the enemy Confederates. And if that man was one of the new African American soldiers, he knew the target on his back was especially large.

There were two flags, or "colors," on every Civil War battlefield. Each had a different meaning to the new African American soldier.

Victory for the Confederate colors meant a continuation of slavery. That was already in the peace platform of the 1864 Democratic Party and its presidential candidate, General George McClellan.[190] Victory for the Confederate flag meant your children and grandchildren would continue to be bought and sold, and your family separated. Your women would continue to be raped, and there was nothing a person could about it.

Victory for the Union colors clearly meant freedom. President Abraham Lincoln said so. And in 1864, the Republicans already filed a constitutional amendment—the Thirteenth Amendment—to ensure that freedom would be permanent everywhere in the United States.[191]

No, those "white men" under the Union colors were not perfect, but at least there was a written agenda and aspiration by the founders to always strive to become "more perfect."

For example, the new African American soldiers had to fight for uniforms and weapons. They fought for equal pay; white solders were paid three dollars more per month.[192] In 1864 Congress passed an equal pay bill for all soldiers, black and white.[193]

And here is one final irony. The African American soldiers had to fight even for the right to fight in the Civil War for their freedom!

---

[190] https://teachingamericanhistory.org/library/document/the-1864-democratic-party-platform/.
[191] https://www.britannica.com/topic/Thirteenth-Amendment.
[192] http://www.freedmen.umd.edu/equalpay.htm.
[193] http://www.freedmen.umd.edu/equalpay.htm.

So that Union flag was special. And to the four men listed at the beginning of this chapter, that Union flag was worth dying for because it stood for freedom, contrary to what is taught in too many universities,.

Answer: The correct answer to the question at the beginning of this *Mercer Moment in American History* is D.

For his actions in 1863, Army Sergeant William Harvey Carney was recognized as the first African American to perform such bravery for which the Medal of Honor was awarded.

William Carney joined the Army in early 1863 as part of the first black-recruited unit of the Union Army, the famous 54th Massachusetts United States Colored Troops.

> Carney was attached to the 54th Massachusetts Colored Infantry. In July 1863, Carney found himself in the fierce Battle of Fort Wagner.
>
> After being wounded, Carney saw that the color bearer had been shot down a few feet away. Carney summoned all his strength to retrieve the fallen colors and continued the charge.
>
> During the charge, Carney was shot several more times, yet he kept the colors flying high. Once delivering the flag back to his regiment, he shouted "The Old Flag never touched the ground!"[194]

I love to challenge and give "homework" to readers. I challenge readers to research Sergeant Carney and the other three men listed at the beginning

---

[194] https://www.army.mil/africanamericans/profiles/carney.html.

of this chapter. I will have another future project, called "Forgotten Americans," that will surely include more about Sergeant William H. Carney.

Finally, let me conclude this chapter with a summary of the Medal of Honor citations for each of the four men listed in this question.

Sergeant William H. Carney

US Army, Company C
54th Massachusetts Colored Infantry
Fort Wagner, South Carolina
July 18, 1863
When the color sergeant was shot down,
this soldier grasped the flag,
led the way to the parapet,
and planted the colors thereon.
When the troops fell back he brought off the flag,
under a fierce fire in which he was twice severely wounded.[195]

First Sergeant Alexander Kelly

US Army, Company F
Division: 6th US Colored Troops
Battle of Chapins Farm, Virginia
September 29, 1864
Gallantly seized the colors,
which had fallen near the enemy's lines of abatis,
raised them and rallied the men at a time of confusion
and in a place of the greatest danger.[196]

---

[195] https://www.cmohs.org/recipients/william-h-carney.

[196] https://www.cmohs.org/recipients/alexander-kelly.

Sergeant Decatur Dorsey

US Army, Company B
Division: 39th US Colored Troops
Battle of the Crater, Petersburg, Virginia
July 30, 1864
Planted his colors on the Confederate
works in advance of his regiment,
and when the regiment was driven back to the Union works
he carried the colors there and bravely rallied the men.[197]

Private Charles Veal

US Army, Company D
Division: 4th US Colored Troops
Battle of the Crater, Petersburg, Virginia
July 30, 1864
Seized the national colors
after 2 color bearers had been shot down
close to the enemy's works,
and bore them through the remainder of the battle.[198]

---

[197] https://www.cmohs.org/recipients/decatur-dorsey.
[198] https://www.cmohs.org/recipients/charles-veal.

*President Abraham Lincoln, with young son Tad and Senator
Charles Sumner, salutes a detachment of African-American Union
troops in Richmond, Virginia at the end of the American Civil War.*

In days to come,
when your son asks you,
"What does this mean?"
say to him,
"With a mighty hand the Lord brought us out of Egypt,
out of the land of slavery."

Exodus 13:14 NIV

14

The Thirteenth Amendment

On January 31, 1865, the US House passed the Thirteenth Amendment to abolish slavery. All eighty-six Republicans voted aye for passage.[199]

Question: In 1865, how many of the sixty-five Democrats in the US House voted for the Thirteenth Amendment?

a) Only 15
b) Over half of the 65
c) All 65
d) None

MMAH Note: Amendments to our US Constitution require passage with a two-thirds majority in both the Senate and House before sending to the states for ratification. Then the process requires three-fourths of the states to ratify the amendment before it will become law.

Many ask with his Emancipation Proclamation ending slavery, why did President Abraham Lincoln and his Republicans require a Thirteenth Amendment to the Constitution?

The proclamation may have applied only to those eleven Confederate states at war at the time. However, there were fifteen Southern states and

---

[199] https://www.govtrack.us/congress/votes/38-2/h480.

The Emancipation Proclamation was an executive order issued by President Abraham Lincoln on January 1, 1863, close to the third year of the American Civil War. The proclamation declared "that all persons held as slaves" within the rebellious states "are, and henceforward shall be free."

other border states that allowed slavery.[200] The Thirteenth Amendment abolished slavery as an institution in every state and territory in our United States.

Here is the text of the 13th Amendment regarding slavery:

Section 1

Neither slavery nor involuntary servitude, except as a punishment for crime whereof the party shall have been duly convicted, shall exist within the United States, or any place subject to their jurisdiction.[201]

Section 2

Congress shall have power to enforce this article by appropriate legislation.[202]

It must be noted that the Thirteenth Amendment superseded article IV, section 2 of our original Constitution. Simply stated, I believe this made any of the old fugitive slave laws illegal.

In April 1864, the US Senate had passed an amendment to abolish slavery with the required two-thirds majority. However, it never moved forward in the House because Democrats were in the middle of an election year and refused to support it.[203] On June 15, 1864, House Democrats defeated the Thirteenth Amendment.[204]

President Abraham Lincoln reacted by putting his whole reelection on the line. He insisted that the passage of the Thirteenth Amendment become a key plank of the 1864 Republican platform.

---

[200] https://www.history.com/topics/black-history/thirteenth-amendment.

[201] https://constitution.congress.gov/constitution/amendment-13/.

[202] https://constitution.congress.gov/constitution/amendment-13/.

[203] https://www.history.com/topics/black-history/thirteenth-amendment.

[204] https://www.govtrack.us/congress/votes/38-1/h348.

Republican Party Platform of 1864

Resolved,
that as slavery was the cause,
and now constitutes the strength of this Rebellion,
and as it must be,
always and everywhere,
hostile to the principles of Republican Government,

justice and the National safety demand
its utter and complete extirpation
from the soil of the Republic;
and that,
while we uphold and maintain
the acts and proclamations
by which the Government,
in its own defense,
has aimed a deathblow at this gigantic evil,
we are in favor,

furthermore,
of such an amendment to the Constitution,
to be made by the people
in conformity with its provisions,
as shall terminate
and forever prohibit
the existence of Slavery
within the limits of the jurisdiction
of the United States.[205]

---

[205] www.presidency.ucsb.edu/documents/republican-party-platform-1864.

Lincoln's presidential reelection campaign was against George B. McClellan, a Democrat and surprisingly, a Union Army major general. McClellan ran on an antiwar platform to end the war and negotiate peace with the Confederate states.[206] Democrats hoped McClellan's popularity with the military would defeat Lincoln.

We in the twenty-first century find it hard to believe that the proslavery Democratic Party was in a strong position to defeat Lincoln in his 1864 reelection bid. All the pollsters had Lincoln losing and losing badly.

In fact, there is an August 23, 1864, memo in the Library of Congress in which Lincoln states, "It seems exceedingly probably that this Administration will not be re-elected."[207]

For the first time in history, absentee voting was allowed in some states. It was restricted to active-duty military. Lincoln supported absentee voting because he hoped the Union Army vote would favor him.[208] But again, Democrats believed the military vote would follow General McClennan.

On Tuesday, November 8, 1864, Abraham Lincoln won the popular vote by only 2.2 million to 1.8 million.[209]

Remember, this was an incredibly unique and historic election because we were a divided nation. The eleven Confederate states (Alabama, Arkansas, Florida, Georgia, Louisiana, Mississippi, North Carolina, South Carolina,

---

[206] https://www.military.com/military-life/how-absentee-voting-us-troops-won-civil-war-and-ended-slavery.html.

[207] http://housedivided.dickinson.edu/sites/lincoln/blind-memorandum-august-23-1864/.

[208] https://www.military.com/military-life/how-absentee-voting-us-troops-won-civil-war-and-ended-slavery.html.

[209] https://www.britannica.com/event/United-States-presidential-election-of-1864.

Tennessee, Texas, and Virginia) did not participate because they claimed Jefferson Davis was their president.[210]

The military vote supported Lincoln with an estimated 70 percent to McClellan's 30 percent. Most important, Lincoln won the 1864 electoral votes by a wide margin, 212–21.[211]

---

[210] https://www.britannica.com/event/United-States-presidential-election-of-1864.
[211] https://www.military.com/military-life/how-absentee-voting-us-troops-won-civil-war-and-ended-slavery.html

1 Edwin M. Stanton   2 Salmon P. Chase   3 Abraham Lincoln   4 Gideon Wells   5 William H. Seward   6 Caleb Smith   7 Montgomery Blair   8 Edwin Bates

THE FIRST READING OF THE EMANCIPATION PROCLAMATION BEFORE THE CABINET

With his reelection, President Lincoln quickly fast-tracked his signature Thirteenth Amendment for passage. Yes, Lincoln became personally involved in the legislative process, using his immense power as president to secure the two-thirds votes needed in the US House.

The legislation was carried by Representative James Ashley, a Republican abolitionist from Ohio. The *Congressional Record* documents that on January 31,1865, the final House vote on the Thirteenth Amendment was 119–56, At 68 percent, it was just barely over the required two-thirds needed for passage.[212], [213]

Those in favor:

- Republicans: all eighty-six
- Democrats: fifteen
- Unconditional Unionists: fourteen
- Union Men: four

Those opposed:

- Democrats: fifty
- Union Men: six

Answer: The correct answer to the question at the beginning of this *Mercer Moment in American History* is A.

Only fifteen of the sixty-five Democrat members of the US House voted for the Thirteenth Amendment to abolish slavery.[214]

---

[212] https://www.history.com/topics/black-history/thirteenth-amendment.

[213] https://www.govtrack.us/congress/votes/38-2/h480.

[214] https://www.govtrack.us/congress/votes/38-2/h480.

MMAH Note: The states then ratified the Third Amendment on December 6, 1865. Sadly, history reminds us that Lincoln never saw the ratification. On April 14, 1865, President Abraham Lincoln was assassinated with a single shot to the back of his head by John Wilkes Booth.[215]

---

[215] https://www.history.com/topics/black-history/thirteenth-amendment.

*President Abraham Lincoln holding the Emancipation
Proclamation and declaring that all persons held as
slaves shall be free, effective as of January 1, 1863.*

He has shown you,
O mortal,
what is good.
And what does the Lord require of you?
To act justly
and to love mercy
and to walk humbly
with your God.

Micah 6:8 NIV

15

The Fifteenth Amendment

In 1870, the Fifteenth Amendment to our US Constitution, which granted African American men the right to vote, was adopted.[216] For passage, a constitutional amendment required two-thirds of the members of both the US House and Senate to vote "Aye."

What percentage of Democrats in the US House and Senate voted for the Fifteenth Amendment?

    a) Zero in both the House and the Senate
    b) 50 percent in the House and 60 percent in the Senate
    c) 60 percent in the House and 75 percent in the Senate
    d) 70 percent in the House and 100 percent in the Senate

---

[216] https://www.history.com/topics/black-history/fifteenth-amendment.

First African-American Vote, 1870. Illustration of Thomas Mundy Peterson, the first African-American to vote in an election, following the newly enacted 15th Amendment to the United States Constitution. His vote was cast on March 31, 1870 in Perth Amboy, New Jersey.

The Fifteenth Amendment to our Constitution was the last of the trilogy of constitutional amendments often referred to as the "Civil War Amendments." This "justice and mercy" trilogy, boldly advanced by Christian abolitionist societies and their leaders—including African American Frederick Douglass—included the abolishment of slavery, the rights of citizenship, and the right to vote.

In 1865, the new Republican Congress passed what eventually became the Civil Rights Act of 1866. The law guaranteed citizenship without regard to a person's race, color, and as stated in the recently ratified Thirteenth Amendment, any previous "condition of slavery or involuntary servitude."[217]

This 1866 act purposely included the rights of African Americans to make and enforce contracts, to sue in a court, to own property, and to receive the equal benefit of all laws, "as is enjoyed by white citizens."[218]

The 1866 civil rights law was critical because many Southern states began passing "black code" laws meant to restrict severely the freedom and privileges of new freedmen. Former African American slaves were forced to work under long contracts with low pay and could not voluntarily change their jobs.[219], [220]

Black code laws prohibited African Americans from owning firearms, and they did not have the right to sue or testify in court. Blacks could be arrested for almost anything, including not having a job. And if they could not pay the fine, they could be bonded for a term of labor.[221], [222]

Without hesitation, Republicans needed to pass the Civil Rights Act of 1866.

---

[217] https://teachingamericanhistory.org/library/document/the-civil-rights-act-of-1866/.

[218] https://teachingamericanhistory.org/library/document/the-civil-rights-act-of-1866/.

[219] https://www.fjc.gov/history/timeline/civil-rights-act-1866.

[220] https://www.britannica.com/topic/black-code.

[221] https://www.britannica.com/topic/black-code.

[222] https://www.history.com/topics/black-history/fourteenth-amendment.

However, with the assassination of Abraham Lincoln, Democrat Andrew Johnson became president. Johnson then vetoed the Civil Rights Act in March 1866.[223] Three weeks after the Johnson veto, the Republicans gained the support for the required two-thirds vote in both the US House and Senate to override Johnson's presidential veto.[224]

This was historic because other than appropriation bills, this was the first time in history that a major piece of legislation was vetoed by the president and then the veto overridden by Congress.[225]

Later in 1866, Congress also adopted the Fourteenth Amendment, which guaranteed citizenship and equal protection under the laws regardless of race. Section 2 of that Amendment punished by reduced representation in the House of Representatives any state that disenfranchised any male citizens over twenty-one years of age.[226], [227]

---

[223] https://history.house.gov/Historical-Highlights/1851-1900/The-Civil-Rights-Bill-of-1866/.

[224] https://history.house.gov/Historical-Highlights/1851-1900/The-Civil-Rights-Bill-of-1866/.

[225] https://www.history.com/topics/black-history/fourteenth-amendment.

[226] https://www.history.com/topics/black-history/fourteenth-amendment.

[227] https://legal-dictionary.thefreedictionary.com/14th+Amendment.

Trilogy of Civil War Amendments

13ᵗʰ Amendment (1865)

Abolish Slavery and Involuntary Servitude

14ᵗʰ Amendment (1868)

Establishes Citizenship, Due Process and
Equal Protection. Reverses 1848 Dred
Scott decision of Supreme Court

15ᵗʰ Amendment (1870)

States cannot deny Citizens the Right to Vote based
on race, color or previous condition of servitude

Even with the passage of the Fourteenth Amendment, the Southern states still believed they possessed the right to deny a ballot to an African American. So the stage was set for the Fifteenth Amendment to guarantee and protect the right to vote. At his presidential Inauguration, Republican Ulysses S. Grant promoted passage of the Fifteenth Amendment.[228, 229, 230]

Much was at stake because the passage could be dangerous and change the political power in the Democrat-controlled South as the states were readmitted to the union. Freed slaves would be rightfully counted 100 percent. Could this change result in increasing the influence for the anti–civil rights Democratic Party?

However, Republicans believed these new African American voters would overwhelming vote Republican. Also, the Republicans had the Union Army staying in the South until the late 1870s to help register and protect these new African American voters.

Extra Credit

What would happen to the registration and protection of the new African American voters after the Union Army left the Southern states?

The Fifteenth Amendment passed with the required two-thirds vote in the US House with 144 Republican votes and no Democratic votes. It then passed in the US Senate with thirty-nine Republican votes and no Democratic votes.[231]

---

[228] https://constitutioncenter.org/interactive-constitution/amendment/amendment-xv.

[229] https://www.history.com/topics/black-history/fifteenth-amendment.

[230] https://www.pbs.org/wgbh/americanexperience/features/grant-fifteenth/.

[231] https://almanacnews.com/square/2015/01/15/how-republicans-and-democrats-voted-on-key-constitutional-amendments.

Answer: The correct answer to this *Mercer Moment in American History* is A.

Zero Democrats from the US House and zero from the US Senate voted for the Fifteenth Amendment to give African American males the right to vote.

Mercer Moment in American History—Further Research

There was a split among female abolitionists who supported the Civil War amendments. They hoped the right to vote for women would also be included in the Fifteenth Amendment. What is the history and result of that split?

With the adoption of the Fifteenth Amendment in 1870, a politically mobilized African American community joined with white Christian supporters in the Southern states to vote the Republican Party in to power. In the next twenty plus years, this brought radical changes across the South, including the election of twenty two African Americans to Congress. They were all Republicans—two senators and twenty members of the House of Representatives.

By late 1870, all the former Confederate states had been readmitted to the Union, and most were controlled by the Republican Party thanks to the support of black voters.

*Portrait of the first African-American Senators and Representatives
in the 41st and 42nd Congress of the United States, 1869-1873.*

16

First African American Member of Congress

Question: Who was the first African American to serve in the US Congress?

a) Tim Scott, South Carolina, Republican
b) Rev. Hiram Rhodes Revels, Mississippi, Republican
c) Blanche Bruce, Mississippi, Republican
d) Edward Brook, Massachusetts, Republican

I remember carrying the motion to add the first African American member of Congress to the US history standards when I served on the Texas State Board of Education. I was surprised that in prior decades, high school and college curriculum experts failed to mention this very important first in our history.

In 2013, Senator Tim Scott, from South Carolina, became that state's first African American senator, but he was not the first in our nation.[232] Senator Tim Scott is included in the above list because I see him as a huge, rising national figure. Watch the career and impact of Senator Scott. I see his star of needed political integrity and leadership as being very, very bright.

Senator Edward Brook of Massachusetts is another possible answer, but not the right one. However, he is especially important because in 1967, he

---

[232] https://history.house.gov/People/Listing/S/SCOTT,-Tim-(S001184)/.

became the first African American to serve in Congress after an eighty-five-year absence of representation.[233]

Beginning in the 1870s, the evil terrorism and racist lynchings of the KKK, along with Jim Crow and black code laws and the voter suppression tactics of literacy tests and the poll tax, combined as a Southern strategy to block the election of another African American to Congress for almost one century. Despite the dramatic oratory of twenty-first-century politicians, history documents that these tactics were all inventions and devices of the Democratic Party to oppress the vote of African Americans in the South.

Senator Brook was the first African American elected to Congress after passage of the Seventeenth Amendment, which allowed direct election by the people. Before the Seventeenth Amendment, the state legislatures determined their US senators.[234] Restated, in 1967, Senator Edward Brook of Massachusetts became the first African American, US Senator elected by "We the People."

Senator Blanche Bruce is another great answer but is again an incorrect response. However, he has two key distinctions. Bruce was selected by the Mississippi legislature and was the first African American to serve a full six-year term as a US Senator.[235, 236]

And equally important, in 1875, Blanche Bruce of Mississippi became the ... only former slave to become a Member of the U.S. Senate.[237]

---

[233] https://history.house.gov/People/Listing/B/BROOKE,-Edward-William,-III-(B000871)/.

[234] https://history.house.gov/People/Listing/B/BROOKE,-Edward-William,-III-(B000871)/.

[235] https://wallbuilders.com/early-black-political-leaders/.

[236] https://history.house.gov/People/Listing/B/BRUCE,-Blanche-Kelso-(B000968)/.

[237] https://wallbuilders.com/early-black-political-leaders/.

Answer: The correct answer to the question at the beginning of this *Mercer Moment in American History* is B.

In 1870, the Mississippi legislature elected Rev. Hiram Rhodes Revels to the US Senate. Senator Revels was the first African American to serve in the US Senate.[238]

The political genre surrounding the era of Rev. Revels was the most unique in our history. After the Civil War, with the passage of the Thirteenth, Fourteenth, and Fifteenth Amendments, Republicans won temporary control of the South.

African American men were free (Thirteenth Amendment), citizens (Fourteenth Amendment), and legally allowed to vote and run for public office (Fifteenth Amendment). In the early years after passage of the 15th Amendment, Republicans sent the Union Army to the South to help register and protect African American men wanting to vote.

However, with the 1865 assassination of President Abraham Lincoln, it was Vice President Andrew Johnson, a Democrat, who became president, and his agenda was not that of Lincoln. Fortunately, the Republicans dominated the House and Senate. They were able to override Johnson's vetoes, including their ability to override his veto of the Fourteenth Amendment. That veto override would become immensely helpful to Rev. Hiram Revels.

Mississippi was readmitted to the Union on February 23, 1870. On February 25 of that same year, Republican Revels was seated as a senator.[239]

Rev. Revels was an ordained minister and religious teacher. During the Civil War he served as a chaplain in the US Army.[240] In 1866 Rev. Revels was called to pastor a church in in Natchez, Mississippi. Two years later, he

---

[238] https://history.house.gov/People/Listing/R/REVELS,-Hiram-Rhodes-(R000166)/.

[239] https://history.house.gov/People/Listing/R/REVELS,-Hiram-Rhodes-(R000166)/.

[240] https://wallbuilders.com/early-black-political-leaders/.

was elected to the Mississippi State Senate, where he was asked to deliver the opening prayer.[241]

This must have been a powerful prayer. Republican State Representative John R. Lynch, a former slave and future member of the US Congress wrote,

> That prayer, one of the most impressive and eloquent prayers that had ever been delivered in the Senate Chamber, made Revels a United States Senator ...[242]

Portraits of African-American heroes, including Blanche Kelso Bruce, Frederick Douglass, and Rev, Hiram Rhoades Revels.

---

[241] https://history.house.gov/People/Listing/R/REVELS,-Hiram-Rhodes-(R000166)/.
[242] https://www.senate.gov/artandhistory/senate-stories/First-African-American-Senator.htm.

Revels was elected by his fellow Mississippi legislators to fill one of two vacant seats in the US Senate. His was an unexpired term when the state seceded from the Union due to the Civil War.[243], [244]

However, Democrats immediately argued a technicality, claiming Revel's short length of time as a "citizen" of the United States disqualified him.[245]

We need to remember that in 1868, the Republicans led the passage of the Fourteenth Amendment, which granted citizenship to people of color, including recently freed slaves. Democrats argued that in 1870, Rev. Hiram Revels had only been a citizen for two years, and that did not meet the requirements to be a US senator.[246]

The Democrats' argument was defeated, and on February 25, 1870, Mississippi gave the United States its first African American member of Congress, Senator Hiram Rhodes Revel of Natchez.[247]

By 1876, due to Democratic white supremist laws, voter suppression tactics, and terrorism of the Southern black codes, Republicans lost their political strength in the South. In was not until the election of 1972 that the next African American members of the US Congress were elected from the South. Democrats Andrew Young of Georgia and Barbara Jordan of Texas became the first blacks in Congress since Reconstruction.

---

[243] https://history.house.gov/People/Listing/R/REVELS,-Hiram-Rhodes-(R000166)/.
[244] https://history.house.gov/Exhibitions-and-Publications/BAIC/Historical-Essays/Fifteenth-Amendment/Introduction/.
[245] https://history.house.gov/People/Listing/R/REVELS,-Hiram-Rhodes-(R000166)/.
[246] https://history.house.gov/People/Listing/R/REVELS,-Hiram-Rhodes-(R000166)/.
[247] https://wallbuilders.com/early-black-political-leaders/.

Mercer Moment in American History: Political Irony

In 1972, Andrew Young and Barbara Jordan were elected to Congress as Southern Democrats, not as Republicans. After a hundred years of terror, lynching, and voter suppression, Republicans had lost their political strength in the South.

Ironically, as we saw in 1860, Democratic majority rulings on landmark Supreme Court decisions—including school prayer (1962) and abortion (1973)—galvanized religious and morality groups and provided a rebirth the Republican Party in 1981, led by eventual Republican president Ronald R. Reagan.

Then you will know the truth,
and the truth will set you free.

—John 8:32 NIV

— 17 —

Arab-Muslim Slave Trade

The transatlantic slave trade and the Arab-Muslim slave trade each targeted the capturing, buying, and selling of slaves. However, little is known and discussed about the Arab-Muslim slave trade.

Question: Which statement is true regarding the Arab-Muslim slave trade?

The Arab-Muslim slave trade

a) Is taught and widely discussed in the schools, colleges, and universities of the United States.
b) Captured, bought, and sold fewer slaves than the thirteen colonies.
c) Did not target female slaves.
d) Did not include white slavery.
e) Was a much more humane form of slavery.
f) All the above are false statements.

Illustration from 19th century of captured and imprisoned Africans.

Truth is always desirable in any serious discussion or debate. In our world regarding slavery and all things related to it, let us make this an opportunity for true peace, resolution, and understanding.

However, truth requires we neither be naïve nor hostile to historical truth and facts. My mother taught me always to ask questions. She wanted me to make sure people were not lying to me or hiding the truth.

In the Texas House of Representatives and the Texas State Board of Education, my reputation was just that—Ken Mercer will ask questions.

Countless times a political or academic expert would testify at a public hearing. And then on completion, some would proudly just walk away from the podium. The chair of that board or committee would then state, "I believe Mr. Mercer has a question."

Mom used to remind me that when you ask so-called experts simple, honest questions and they get mad, it usually means, "You are asking the right questions." They are hiding something. They are afraid of the truth.

What is the truth of the Arab-Muslim slave trade in Africa? Why have so many experts in our colleges and universities censored that part of history about slavery?

Ghanaian professor and minister John Allembillah Azumah was the director of the Centre of Islamic Studies at the London School of Theology.[248] He addresses this subject in his book *The Legacy of Arab-Islam in Africa*.

Born a Muslim and later converted to Christianity, Dr. Azumah earned his PhD in Islamic studies from Birmingham University in the United Kingdom.[249] Dr. Azumah is concerned about the efforts of American universities to demonize and place all blame for slavery on only Western civilization while romanticizing what they refer to as the "Golden Age of Islam."[250]

---

[248] https://berkleycenter.georgetown.edu/people/john-azumah.

[249] https://berkleycenter.georgetown.edu/people/john-azumah.

[250] https://adarapress.com/2016/09/14/comparing-the-islamic-slave-to-the-american-slave-trade-the-legacy-of-arab-islam-in-africa-dr-john-azumah-video/.

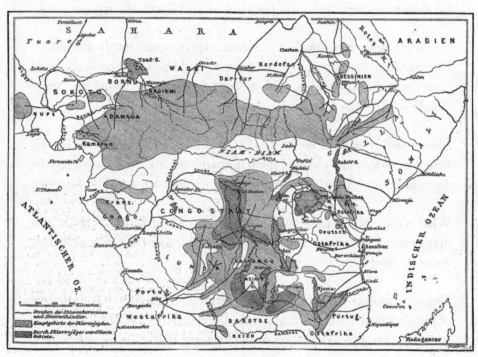

The territories of the 19th century African Slave Trade.

There is an excellent 2020 column in the *Toronto Sun* by attorney and best-selling author Larry Elder titled, "Why Don't They Teach about the Arab-Muslim Slave Trade in Africa?" Elder, a nationally recognized, African American radio talk show host, remarks,

> Despite years of Black History Februarys, many know little to nothing about the vast role played by Arab and Muslim slavers in the African slave trade.

> The practice began centuries before Europeans slavers bought and transported slaves out of Africa and continued well after European slavery ended.[251]

Dr. Sheldon M. Stern was a college professor for a decade. He later designed the first civil rights exhibit for the John F. Kennedy Library and Museum. Dr. Stern studied the US history curriculum standards for each state and found that forty-nine states had no mention of the role of powerful African tribes in capturing and supplying the Trans-Atlantic slave trade.[252]

There are African nations that teach about the African slave trade differently than it is taught in the United States. Here is one example of what Nigerians teach about their role in the slave trade of fellow Africans:

> Where did the supply of slaves come from? First, the Portuguese themselves kidnapped some Africans.

> But the bulk of the supply came from the Nigerians.

> These Nigerian middlemen moved to the interior where they captured other Nigerians who belonged to other communities. The middlemen also purchased many of the slaves from the people in the interior ...

---

[251] https://www.larryelder.com/column/black-history-month-why-dont-they-teach-about-the-arab-muslim-slave-trade-in-africa/.
[252] https://historynewsnetwork.org/article/41431#_edn5.

Many Nigerian middlemen began to depend totally on the slave trade and neglected every other business and occupation.

The result was that when the trade was abolished [by England in 1807] these Nigerians began to protest. As years went by and the trade collapsed such Nigerians lost their sources of income and became impoverished.[253]

Dr. Stern cites an article from the *New York Times* that included remarks from Samuel Sulemana Fuseini, a politician and educator from the African nation of Ghana.

Samuel Sulemana Fuseini has acknowledged that his Asante ancestors accumulated their great wealth by abducting, capturing, and kidnapping Africans and selling them as slaves.[254]

The *Atlanta Black Star,* in a 2014 article, "10 Facts about the Arab Enslavement of Black People Not Taught in Schools,"stated the following:

Some historians estimate that between A.D. 650 and 1900, 10 million to 20 million people were enslaved by Arab slave traders. Others believe over 20 million enslaved Africans alone had been delivered through the trans-Saharan route alone to the Islamic world.

I will end this section with a quote and citation from Dr. Stern's research regarding a former diplomat of Ghana, Kofi Awoonor:

---

[253] Michael Omolewa, *Certificate History of Nigeria* (Lagos, Nigeria: Longman Group, 1991), 96–103, cited in Dana Lindaman and Kyle Ward, *History Lessons: How Textbooks around the World Portray U.S. History* (New York: New Press, 2004), 79–83.
[254] Johnson et al., *Africans in America,* 2–3; Howard W. French, "On Slavery, Africans Say the Guilt Is Theirs, Too," *New York Times,* 27 December 1994, A4.

African men, women, and children who were rescued by the
British navy from a slaving vessel in 1884. Two British sailors
from the HMS Undine are seen in the background. Although
the slave trade was abolished in many countries during the
19th century, slave trading continued in other countries.

> I believe there is a great psychic shadow over Africa, and it has much to do with our guilt and denial of our role in the slave trade. We too are blameworthy in what was essentially one of the most heinous crimes in human history.[255]

Finally, yes there are academics from Africa who are concerned that American publishers are not showing any interest in their firsthand accounts, primary-source studies and research regarding the Arab-Muslim slave trade.

Answer: False. The Arab-Muslim slave trade is not taught or widely discussed in the schools, colleges, and universities of the United States.

My Christian colleagues understand that a lie is usually an outright falsehood. In the academic world, a lie is purposely censuring known truth.

True or False: The Arab-Muslim slave trade captured, bought, and sold fewer slaves than the thirteen colonies.

Academic sources estimate between 390,000 and 550,000 African slaves arrived in the original thirteen colonies due to the transatlantic slave trade. This means 4 to 5 percent of the 11 million African slaves transported across the Atlantic Ocean came to North America, and 95 percent or more went to South America and the Caribbean.

Specifically, Dr. Azumah, in an interview, shared,

> It is estimated that possibly as many as 11 million Africans were transported across the Atlantic, 95% of which went to South and Central America, mainly to Portuguese, Spanish and French possessions; only 5% of the slaves ended up in what we call the United States today.

---

[255] Johnson et al., *Africans in America*, 2–3; Howard W. French, "On Slavery, Africans Say the Guilt Is Theirs, Too," *New York Times*, 27 December 1994, A4.

However, a minimum of 28 million Africans were enslaved in the Muslim Middle East.[256]

Dr. Azumah believes at least 28 million Africans survived the transportation as slaves to the Middle East, fifty times more that those who arrived in the thirteen colonies.

Again, there are estimates that 80 percent of the Africans captured by the Muslim slave traders died before reaching the slave markets. This means the real number is much higher than 28 million Africans.[257]

Using simple math, divide the high estimate (550,000) for the thirteen colonies and divide by the low estimate (28,000,000) of Africans for the Arab-Muslim slave trade, and your answer is 2 percent, or one fiftieth.

Answer: False. The Arab-Muslim slave trade did not capture, buy, and sell fewer slaves than the thirteen colonies.

In fact, a conservative estimate is that the Arab-Muslim form of slavery captured, bought, and sold fifty times more slaves than the thirteen colonies.

True or False: The Arab-Muslim slave trade did not target female slaves.

The transatlantic trade between Africa and the Americas put a high value on males for agricultural work. Two of every three captured slaves were male. What was the ratio for females in the Arab-Muslim trade?

Dr. John Azumah explains the ratio for the Arab-Muslim trade was reversed:

---

[256] https://adarapress.com/2016/09/14/comparing-the-islamic-slave-to-the-american-slave-trade-the-legacy-of-arab-islam-in-africa-dr-john-azumah-video/.
[257] https://adarapress.com/2016/09/14/comparing-the-islamic-slave-to-the-american-slave-trade-the-legacy-of-arab-islam-in-africa-dr-john-azumah-video/.

*A group of African slaves paddling a piroque which is carrying
an Arab slave-dealer across a body of water. Other boats can
be seen in the background, similarly crewed. The slave dealer
is probably taking the slaves to a slave market to sell them.*

141

While two out of every three slaves shipped across the Atlantic were men, the proportions were reversed in the Islamic slave trade. Two women for every man were enslaved by the Muslims.[258, 259]

The *Atlantic Black Star* validates the analysis of Dr. Azumah:

The eastern Arab slave trade dealt primarily with African women, maintaining a ratio of two women for each man. These women and young girls were used by Arabs and other Asians as concubines and menials.

A Muslim slaveholder was entitled by law to the sexual enjoyment of his slave women. Filling the harems of wealthy Arabs, African women bore them a host of children.

This abuse of African women would continue for nearly 1,200 years.[260]

British writer Duncan Clarke shares this view in the *New African Magazine*: "Thus, women slaves in the Arab world were often turned into concubines living in harems, and rarely as wives."[261] Mr. Clarke believes the ratio of females over males in the Arab-Muslim slave trade may be closer to three-to-one.

Naiwu Osahon is a renowned author and recognized leader of the world Pan-African Movement. His studies on Arab enslavement reported:

---

[258] https://torontosun.com/opinion/columnists/elder-why-dont-they-teach-about-the-arab-muslim-slave-trade.
[259] https://atlantablackstar.com/2014/06/02/10-facts-about-the-arab-enslavement-of-black-people-not-taught-in-schools/2/.
[260] https://atlantablackstar.com/2014/06/02/10-facts-about-the-arab-enslavement-of-black-people-not-taught-in-schools/2/.
[261] https://newafricanmagazine.com/16616/.

The African male slaves were castrated and used as domestic servants or to work the Sahara salt deposits or on farms all over the Islamic world. The African female servants were continuously raped before being sold to households to be used as sex labour.[262]

The *New African Magazine* provides this "real face" of female slavery:

In modern times, the popular image of African slavery springs from the vision of a tormented male suffering under the lash of unceasing labour on some 'New World' sugar plantation.

Yet the real face of servitude finds its focus in the forced migration of millions of girls and young women across the Sahara and the Horn of Africa in to the institutions of Islamic concubinage.[263]

Finally, Dr. Azumah emphasizes,

While almost all the slaves shipped across the Atlantic were for agricultural work, most of the slaves destined for the Muslim Middle East were for sexual exploitation as concubines in harems and for military service.[264]

Answer: False. The Arab-Muslim slave trade did target female slaves.

True or False: The Arab-Muslim slave trade did not include white slavery.

---

[262] https://nigeriachristiangraduatefellowshipblog.wordpress.com/arabs-mortal-hatred-and-enslavement-of-africa/.

[263] https://newafricanmagazine.com/16616/.

[264] https://adarapress.com/2016/09/14/comparing-the-islamic-slave-to-the-american-slave-trade-the-legacy-of-arab-islam-in-africa-dr-john-azumah-video/.

Here is one perspective that we never asked. Is the history of slavery, in this case Arab -Muslim slavery, limited only to people of color?

Professor Robert Davis of Ohio State University calculated that between the years 1530 and 1780, between 1 million and 1.25 million white, European Christians were captured and enslaved by the Muslims of the Barbary Coast.[265] Khaled Diab, a renowned Egyptian-Belgian journalist, collaborates Davis's study in his op-ed to Al Jazeera with the same number of more than 1 million white Christian Europeans captured and sold by Muslin pirates in the same period.[266]

The BBC documents that between the years 1609 and 1616, Barbary "corsairs" (pirates for the Barbary Coast of Africa) with the authorization of their coast of Africa governments, captured and plundered at least 466 ships and sold the sailors into slavery.[267] The Muslim slave raids then extended into the small coastal villages of England, Spain, Italy, and other Europeans counties.

> A conservative estimate is that between the years 1580 and 1680, over 850,000 white, Christian, European children, women, and men were captured and sold into slavery. By the year 1780, the number may have increased to as high as 1,250,000 slaves.[268]

Larry Elder refers us to a quote from a renowned African American economist, Dr. Thomas Sowell, regarding white slavery. As mentioned previously, Dr. Sowell is a Senior Fellow at the Hoover Institution of Stanford University.[269]

---

[265] https://news.osu.edu/when-europeans-were-slaves--research-suggests-white-slavery-was-much-more-common-than-previously-believed/.

[266] https://www.aljazeera.com/indepth/opinion/2015/05/slaves-history-baltimore-150505082953176.html.

[267] http://www.bbc.co.uk/history/british/empire_seapower/white_slaves_01.shtml.

[268] http://www.bbc.co.uk/history/british/empire_seapower/white_slaves_01.shtml.

[269] https://www.thefamouspeople.com/profiles/thomas-sowell-3032.php.

More whites were brought as slaves to North Africa than blacks brought as slaves to the United States or to the 13 colonies from which it was formed.

White slaves were still being bought and sold in the Ottoman Empire, decades after blacks were freed in the United States.[270]

Answer: False. The Arab-Muslim slave trade did include white slavery.

---

[270] https://torontosun.com/opinion/columnists/elder-why-dont-they-teach-about-the-arab-muslim-slave-trade.

Bishop Crowther.

Vintage photograph of Bishop Samuel Ajayi Crowther, the first African Anglican bishop in Nigeria. He was 12 years old when he was captured, along with his mother and toddler brother and other family members, along with his entire village, by Muslim Fulani slave raiders in 1821 and sold to Portuguese slave traders. Before leaving port, his ship was boarded by a Royal Navy ship under the command of Captain Henry Leeke, and Crowther was taken to Freetown, Sierra Leone and released.

True or False: The Arab-Muslim slave trade is a much more humane slave trade.

British writer Duncan Clarke tells us that male slaves and young boys were castrated and had their male sex organs manipulated. They were sold in a very profitable market as eunuchs, who kept watch over the harems.[271] Clarke estimates that the survival rate for young boys and men of this horrible operation was only 10 percent.[272] That means for every one "live" eunuch, nine perished. It seems the slave market for eunuchs was so profitable, this grossly inhumane loss was acceptable.

The *Atlanta Black Star* corroborates this with a statement of boys between the ages of eight and twelve having their male organs completely amputated to become a eunuch and prevent them from reproducing. This account has a minimum of 60 percent of the captured boy slaves bleeding to death from the procedure.

Author Ronald Segal, in his book *Islam's Black Slaves: The Other Black Diaspora*, provides this example regarding eunuchs: "The caliph in Baghdad at the beginning of the 10th Century had 7,000 black eunuchs and 4,000 white eunuchs in his palace."[273]

Let us do the horrid math. In Muslim governments, a caliph is the political leader. This caliph had 11,000 eunuchs who survived the castration and genital manipulation when captured as young boys. If 60 percent to 90 percent of captured male slaves perished due to the operations on their male anatomy, that means the caliph had to capture and enslave 27,500 to 110,000 young boys to eventually produce 11,000 eunuchs.

I will close this painful chapter of truth with two quotes from Dr. John Azumah:

---

[271] https://newafricanmagazine.com/16616/.

[272] https://newafricanmagazine.com/16616/.

[273] https://atlantablackstar.com/2014/06/02/10-facts-about-the-arab-enslavement-of-black-people-not-taught-in-schools/2/.

While the mortality rate of the slaves being transported across the Atlantic was as high as 10%, the percentage of the slaves dying in transit in the Tran-Saharan and East African slave market was a staggering 80 to 90%.

However, a minimum of 28 million Africans were enslaved in the Muslim Middle East. Since at least 80% of those captured by the Muslim slave traders were calculated to have died before reaching the slave markets, it is believed that the death toll from 1,400 years of Arab and Muslim slave raids into Africa could have been as high as 112 million.[274]

Answer: The correct answer to this *Mercer Moment in American History* is F, all the above. Statements A through E are false.

Statements A–E minimize or even romanticize the Arab-Muslim slave trade.

---

[274] https://www.bing.com/videos/search?q=john+azumah+&&view=detail &mid=BB3E174FB0E8016E4ADCBB3E174FB0E8016E4ADC&&FORM= VRDGAR&ru=%2Fvideos%2Fsearch%3Fq%3Djohn%2520azumah%2520%26q s%3Dn%26form%3DQBVR%26sp%3D-1%26pq%3Djohn%2520azumah%2520 %26sc%3D6-12%26sk%3D%26cvid%3DB94E506B843642FCAE86473A64CA 17F1.

Door of No Return – Slave Monument – Quidah, Benin

18

Last Nation to Abolish Slavery

Great Britain abolished the Atlantic slave trade" in 1807 and abolished slavery in all British colonies in 1833. The United States abolished slavery in 1865 with Lincoln's Emancipation Proclamation and the states' ratification of the Thirteenth Amendment to our Constitution.

Question: Which was the last nation on earth to abolish, at least on paper, the practice of slavery?

  a)   Mauritania
  b)   Saudi Arabia
  c)   Yemen
  d)   Qatar
  e)   United Arab Emirates (UAE)

Slavery was abolished in the United States in 1865, after the Civil War. The agenda of political revisionists fails to teach our college students that slavery remained legal in many countries of the world for more than a hundred years.

Historical accuracy points to the five nations listed previously as being the last countries to formally legislate, at least on paper, the abolishment of slavery.

But is slavery gone in our twenty-first-century world? No.

I remember leading the fight against the indoctrination in education of something called "Common Core." I was proud when my friends in the Texas legislature passed a law to abolish it. However, those well-intentioned lawmakers provided no teeth to the law, meaning there was no punishment or penalty for those who continued teaching it.

So though Common Core was technically abolished in Texas, I sat through four years of official state hearings where parents repeatedly testified that with no ability to enforce the law, Common Core still existed and was taught in many areas of our state.

I apply the same analogy to twenty-first-century worldwide slavery. It is my belief that at least half of the 191 member states of the United Nations that abolished slavery have failed to pass any laws to criminalize and enforce that abolishment.

It is interesting to note that the last five countries in our world to abolish slavery formally are each considered an Arab state. The information presented below is from the 2018 Global Slavery Index (GSI), and the source for analysis is www.globalslaveryindex.org.[275]

It must be noted that the GSI website includes this important note:

> Substantial gaps in data exist for the Arab States region and Gulf countries in particular. These gaps point to a significant underestimate of the extent of modern slavery in this region.
>
> As a result, the country-level estimates presented here are considered very conservative and should be interpreted cautiously."

Qatar formally abolished slavery in 1952. However, the GSI estimated in 2018 there were still at least four thousand victims of slavery in this small

---

[275] https://www.globalslaveryindex.org/2018/findings/global-findings/.

country. The GSI for Qatar in 2018 was 1.5 slaves per 1,000 persons. Qatar became a member of the United Nations in 1971.

In 1962, slavery was formally abolished in Yemen. The GSI estimated in 2018 there remained 85,000 victims of slavery. The GSI for Yemen in 2018 was 3.1 persons per 1,000. Yemen became a member of the United Nations in 1947.

Saudi Arabia also abolished slavery in 1962. The GSI estimated in 2018 there were 61,000 victims of slavery. The GSI for Saudi Arabia in 2018 was 1.9 persons per 1,000. Saudi Arabia became a member of the United Nations in 1945.

In 1963 slavery was formally abolished in the United Arab Emirates. The GSI estimated in 2018 there are 15,000 victims of slavery. The GSI for the UAE is 1.7 persons per 1,000. The United Arab Emirates became a member of the United Nations in 1971.[276]

In 1981, the northwestern African county of Mauritania officially became the last country in the world to abolish the practice of slavery. However, it was not until 2007, after international rebuke and pressure, that the government of Mauritania finally passed a law that allowed slaveholders to be prosecuted.

In 2018, the GSI gave a very conservative estimate of 90,000 people, or 2.2 percent of the 4.1 million people in Mauritania, living in slavery. Mauritania has been a member of the United Nations since 1961.[277]

How conservative is the GSI? In 2017, the BBC estimated 600,000, or 15 percent, of Mauritania's population lives in some form of bonded labor. The GSI and BBC both agree that Mauritania has the highest percentage of people in slavery of any country in the world. These slaves are largely a black population enslaved by Arab masters.[278]

---

[276] https://www.globalslaveryindex.org/2018/findings/regional-analysis/arab-states/.

[277] https://www.globalslaveryindex.org/2018/data/country-data/mauritania/.

[278] http://www.bbc.co.uk/worldservice/specials/1458_abolition/page4.shtml.

Amnesty International supports the analysis. And in terms of enforcement of the abolishment, some global human rights groups claim the Muslim-dominated government of Mauritania may have jailed more antislavery activists than slave owners.

Here is one response of Mauritania regarding the talk of slavery in their country: " ... suggests manipulation by the West, an act of enmity toward Islam, or influence from the worldwide Jewish conspiracy."

According to the US State Department, abuses in Mauritania include:

> ... mistreatment of detainees and prisoners; security force impunity; lengthy pretrial detention; harsh prison conditions;

> arbitrary arrests; limits on freedom of the press and assembly; corruption;

> discrimination against women; female genital mutilation (FGM); child marriage;

> political marginalization of southern-based ethnic groups; racial and ethnic discrimination; slavery and slavery-related practices; and child labor.[279]

The report continues,

> Government efforts were not sufficient to enforce the antislavery law. No cases have been successfully prosecuted under the antislavery law despite the fact that 'de facto' slavery exists in Mauritania.[280]

---

[279] "Slavery in Mauritania: An Overview and Action Plan." Archived 5 November 2013 at the Wayback Machine, United States Embassy in Nouakchott.
[280] "Slavery in Mauritania: An Overview and Action Plan." Archived 5 November 2013 at the Wayback Machine, United States Embassy in Nouakchott.

_____

_____

Answer: The correct answer to this *Mercer Moment in American History* is A.

In 1981, the northwest African nation of Mauritania became the last country in the world to abolish slavery officially.

Here is a quick timeline of the last five countries to abolish slavery

- 1981 Mauritania
- 1963 United Arab Emirates (UAE)
- 1962 Saudi Arabia
- 1962 Yemen
- 1952 Qatar

I conclude this question and chapter with a factual reminder to certain "anti-America" college professors whose political agenda and research methods are suspect. Again, slavery was legally abolished by the United States of America in 1865, almost a hundred years before these five nations did so.

And I believe the United States may be the only nation on earth to go to a Civil War with the result being the emancipation of slaves. Approximately 360,000 Union soldiers made the ultimate sacrifice that led to the rightful abolition of slavery and freedom for 4 million African Americans.

The following is an argument by Frederick Douglass opposing the plan of the American Colonization Society (ACS). The ACS supported the repatriation/migration for freed African Americans to Liberia in Africa. However, they might be captured and sold again.

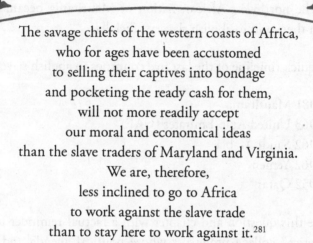

The savage chiefs of the western coasts of Africa,
who for ages have been accustomed
to selling their captives into bondage
and pocketing the ready cash for them,
will not more readily accept
our moral and economical ideas
than the slave traders of Maryland and Virginia.
We are, therefore,
less inclined to go to Africa
to work against the slave trade
than to stay here to work against it.[281]

—Frederick Douglass,
Ordained Minister AME Zion Church,
Gifted Orator, Abolitionist, Freedman
Counsel to Presidents Abraham Lincoln and Ulysses S. Grant
on equal rights, civil rights, voting rights, the Emancipation
Proclamation, and the Thirteenth Amendment, Fourteenth
Amendment, and Fifteenth Amendment to the Constitution.

[281] https://historynewsnetwork.org/article/125861

19

Worst and Best in the Twenty-First Century

In 2018, the highest documented rates of human slavery continue to remain in countries from the continents of Africa and Asia.

Question: Which country has the highest rate (human slaves per 1,000 population) of slavery in the world?

a) Eritrea, Africa
b) Sudan, Africa
c) Burundi, Africa
d) Iran
e) North Korea
f) Democrat Republic of the Congo, Africa

Again, I must repeat that human slavery is EDS—evil, demonic, and satanic. For some reason, politicians forget to mention that slavery still occurs today in the very same regions that profited in the 1800s from the horrific transatlantic slave trade.

Why does slavery still exist, and is it still accepted?

In 2019 US House Speaker Nancy Pelosi (D-California) and twelve Democrats traveled to Ghana, Africa, to commemorate the 1619 anniversary of the first slaves from Africa arriving in Jamestown, Virginia.[282]

Some politicians do not seem to know about the past involvement in the slave trade of powerful African tribes and that today there are 9.2 million slaves in Africa.

The GSI (https://www.globalslaveryindex.org) tells us,

> On any given day in 2016, an estimated 9.2 million men, women, and children were living in modern slavery in Africa. The region has the highest rate of prevalence, with 7.6 people living in modern slavery for every 1,000 people in the region.[283]

Dr. Henry Louis Gates, professor at Harvard University, agrees: "Today in Africa there are an estimated 9.2-million people living in modern day slavery, but Western politicians do not speak out against this injustice."[284, 285]

If Democrats and Republicans are serious about eliminating the evil sin of twenty-first-century slavery, they will want to begin with modern-day Africa.

In the twenty-first century, these are the top areas of concern I found for modern-day slavery: [286, 287]

---

[282] https://www.thegatewaypundit.com/2019/07/never-forget-388000-slaves-were-sent-to-america-from-1525-to-1866-but-today-there-are-still-9-2-million-slaves-in-africa-alone/.

[283] https://www.globalslaveryindex.org/2018/findings/regional-analysis/africa/.

[284] https://www.thegatewaypundit.com/2019/07/never-forget-388000-slaves-were-sent-to-america-from-1525-to-1866-but-today-there-are-still-9-2-million-slaves-in-africa-alone/.

[285] https://hutchinscenter.fas.harvard.edu/henry-louis-gates-jr.

[286] http://www.endslaverynow.org/learn/slavery-today.

[287] https://www.state.gov/what-is-modern-slavery/.

- Sex trafficking
- Child sex trafficking
- Forced adult labor, bonded labor, or debt bondage
- Domestic servitude (workers in private homes convinced that they have no option to leave)
- Unlawful recruitment and use of child soldiers
- Child labor
- Forced marriage

As witnessed before, during the American Civil War regarding slavery, I believe once again our Ephesians 6 women and men of faith are ready to "put on their full armor" to fight to abolish and finally eradicate worldwide slavery.

While financial reparations may be an interesting discussion, any political blame game may in reality be only an election device.

The real questions must be: "Where does human slavery exists today?" "Why does it exist?" "How do we forever stop it?" To blame solely white Europeans for a system of slavery that existed for 850 years prior to 1619, and then continued for 155 years after 1865, fails to answer those questions.

For example, why does history show us that these same white Europeans who purchased African slaves then became the first nations (both the United Kingdom and the United States) in the world to abolish slavery? I believe the answer is that "the church" finally became the church!

Abolitionist Frederick Douglass complained about southern "White churches" that either supported slavery or chose to remain silent on the issue.[288] Northern Christian churches dramatically changed the culture with seventy-five years of evangelical revivals. It was that powerful wave of change called the Great Awakening in the United Kingdom and the United States that birthed the movement to abolish slavery.

---

[288] https://www.christianitytoday.com/ct/2018/january-february/frederick-douglass-at-200-remembering-his-radical-christian.html.

However, what happened to abolishment of slavery by the African and Asia countries?

Why after the War of 1812 did the Royal (British) Navy and the US Navy agree to work together for forty-plus years of joint operations as antislavery patrols, which were to end the Atlantic slave trade along the huge, 3,000-mile coast of West Africa?[289], [290] We need to know that before the United States Civil War of 1860, our navy was conducting joint antislavery operations along the coast of West Africa with the British.[291]

However, because too many of the powerful African tribal leaders were opposed, the operation became exceedingly difficult.

In the 1830s, the British became highly active in abolishing the slavery. They sent diplomatic parties to the Kingdom of Dahomey (present-day Benin) to demand they end the practice of capturing and selling slaves. Why did Dahomey refuse? Let us consider a few perceptive remarks from Dr. Gates:

> While we are all familiar with the role played by the United States and the European colonial powers like Britain, France, Holland, Portugal and Spain, there is very little discussion of the role Africans themselves played.
>
> And that role, it turns out, was a considerable one, especially for the slave-trading kingdoms of western and central Africa. These included the Akan of the kingdom of Asante in what is now Ghana, the Fon of Dahomey (now Benin), the Mbundu of Ndongo in modern Angola and the Kongo of today's Congo, among several others.[292]

---

[289] https://www.forces.net/services/tri-service/how-royal-navy-helped-stop-slave-trade.

[290] http://www.bbc.co.uk/history/british/abolition/royal_navy_article_01.shtml.

[291] https://www.history.navy.mil/content/history/museums/nmusn/explore/exhibits/anti-slave-trade-patrols.html.

[292] https://historynewsnetwork.org/article/125861.

In fact, the nation of Benin is a good example of recognizing the role of powerful African tribal leaders in capturing, buying, and selling fellow Africans. The *Chicago Tribune* (May 1, 2020) reported:

> Officials from the West African nation Benin apologized during a ceremony here for their country's role in once selling fellow Africans by the millions to white slave traders.[293]

The *Tribune News Service* quoted Luc Gnacadja, the Benin minister of Environment and Housing as stating, "We cry for forgiveness and reconciliation," and later, "The slave trade is a shame, and we do repent for it."[294]

The *Washington Post* (January 29, 2018) describes a 1999 speech by Benin's president Mathieu Kerekou at an all-black church in Baltimore, Maryland:

> Falling to his knees and begging African-Americans' forgiveness for the 'shameful' and 'abominable' role Africans played in the trade."[295]

The *Washington Post* continued,

> For over 200 years, powerful kings in what is now the country of Benin captured and sold slaves to Portuguese, French and British merchants. The slaves were usually men, women and children from rival tribes—gagged and jammed into boats bound for Brazil, Haiti and the United States.[296]

---

[293] https://www.chicagotribune.com/news/ct-xpm-2000-05-01-0005010158-story.html.

[294] https://www.chicagotribune.com/news/ct-xpm-2000-05-01-0005010158-story.html.

[295] https://www.washingtonpost.com/world/africa/an-african-country-reckons-with-its-history-of-selling-slaves/2018/01/29/5234f5aa-ff9a-11e7-86b9-8908743c79dd_story.html.

[296] https://www.washingtonpost.com/world/africa/an-african-country-reckons-with-its-history-of-selling-slaves/2018/01/29/5234f5aa-ff9a-11e7-86b9-8908743c79dd_story.html.

The African role in the slave trade was fully understood and openly acknowledged by many African Americans even before the Civil War. For example. there were those who wanted the United States to fund the return, or "repatriation," of former slaves to return home to Africa. It is interesting how abolitionist, Christian minister, and gifted orator Frederick Douglass responded:

> The savage chiefs of the western coasts of Africa, who for ages have been accustomed to selling their captives into bondage, and pocketing the ready cash for them will not more readily accept our moral and economical ideas than the slave traders of Maryland and Virginia.[297]

The recognition of the past sins on both sides must translate into positive and meaningful change in the future. Yes, Africa has a long history of slave trading, including the Arab-Muslim and the transatlantic slave trade, but what about in the twenty-first century?

Africa and Asia still lead the world in modern-day slavery. Unfortunately there are governments that abolished slavery in name only and still refuse to take real action.

The chart ending this chapter leaves us with a thousand questions but presents a clear understanding of the magnitude of the problem politicians refuse to acknowledge.

Answer: The answer to this question in *Mercer Moment in American History* is E, North Korea.

In 2018, the GSI points to North Korea as having 2.64 million people living in slavery. The population of North Korea was estimated at 25.24

---

[297] https://historynewsnetwork.org/article/125861.

million. The GSI is 104.5 per 1,000 persons, meaning that North Korea is the worst in the world with 104 slaves per every 1,000 persons.[298]

The GSI's investigation of slavery throughout the world included 167 nations.

Note each nation's:

- Slavery rank, with 1 being the worst in the world
- Persons living in slavery per 1,000
- Government response to slavery rating

---

[298] https://www.globalslaveryindex.org/2018/findings/global-findings/.

Government Response Rating Chart (AAA is best)[299]

AAA	AA	A	BBB	BB	B	CCC	CC	C	D

Note the GSI cautions that these figures are very conservative numbers as they are based only on the data these nations allow to be collected for analysis.

Fifteen Nations Rated Worst/Most Dangerous for Modern-Day Slavery[300]

Nation	Continent	Slavery Rank, 167 Nations, 1 = worst)	Persons Living in Slavery per 1,000	Estimated Number of Slaves	Government Response to Slavery Rating
North Korea	Asia	1	104.56	2,640,000	D
Eritrea	Africa	2	93.03	451,000	D
Burundi	Africa	3	39.95	408,000	C
Central African Rep	Africa	4	22.25	101,000	D
Afghanistan	Asia	5	22.19	749,000	*
Mauritania	Africa	6	21.43	90,000	C
South Sudan	Africa	7	20.46	243,000	*
Pakistan	Asia	8	16.82	3,186,000	C
Cambodia	Asia	9	16.81	261,000	CCC
Iran	Asia	10	16.24	1,289,000	D
Somalia	Africa	11	15.50	216,000	C
Dem Rep of Congo	Africa	12	13.71	1,045,000	C
Mongolia	Asia	13	12.29	37,000	CCC
Sudan	Africa	14	12.04	465,000	C
Chad	Africa	15	11.98	168,000	C

*Due to ongoing conflict and extreme disruption to government, unable to include a rating.

---

[299] https://www.globalslaveryindex.org/2018/findings/global-findings/.
[300] https://www.globalslaveryindex.org/2018/findings/global-findings/.

Finally, I promised to identify which twenty-first-century nations are the best in their efforts to combat modern slavery. Using the 2018 data from the same GSI, the following are the "top-10" nations recognized for their policies and laws to end modern-day slavery.[301]

Through my analysis I added the columns labeled "Continent" and "Majority Religion." It is interesting to note the predominant majority religion in those nations with the best records of fighting and abolishing modern slavery is Christianity.

---

[301] https://www.globalslaveryindex.org/2018/findings/global-findings/.

Slavery Fortress on Goree Island, off the coast of Senegal. From the 15th to the 19th century, it was the largest slave-trading center on the African coast.

Top Ten Nations Rated Best for Fighting/
Abolishing Modern-Day Slavery[302]

Nation	Continent	Rank of 167 Nations (167 = Best)	Majority Religion	Living in Slavery per 1,000	Government Slavery Response Rating
United States	North America	158	Christianity	1.26	BBB
Costa Rica	North America	159	Christianity	1.25	BB
Uruguay	South America	160	Christianity	1.03	BB
Mauritius	Africa	161	Hindu/ Christian	1.0	CCC
Chile	South America	162	Christianity	0.78	BBB
Australia	Australia	163	Christianity	0.65	BBB
New Zealand	Zealandia	164	Christianity	0.64	BB
Taiwan	Asia	165	Buddhism/ Taoism	0.49	CC
Canada	North America	166	Christianity	0.48	BB
Japan	Asia	167	Shinto / Buddhism	0.29	CCC

---

[302] https://www.globalslaveryindex.org/2018/findings/global-findings/.

Upon the outbreak of the Civil War,
black Americans
—both slave and free—
believed that God would use
President Abraham Lincoln and General Ulysses S. Grant
to bring them freedom in the same way that
God had used Moses to lead the Israelites out of captivity.
Viewing abolition as a spiritual mission
made black Americans all the more eager to help,
thereby hastening the arrival of freedom.[303]

—David Barton, WallBuilders

[303] https://wallbuilders.com/black-history-issue-2006/.

20

First "Civil Rights President"

In the nineteenth and twentieth centuries, several landmark pieces of civil rights legislation were passed.

Who was considered the first "civil rights president"?

a) Sixteenth president—Abraham Lincoln
b) Seventeenth president—Andrew Johnson
c) Thirty-sixth president—Lyndon B. Johnson
d) Eighteenth president—Ulysses S. Grant

In this final chapter, I am reminded that in our United States, our civil rights are those guarantees of equal social opportunities and equal protection under the law. These are guarantees regardless of your race, religion, or other personal characteristics.[304]

During the Civil War, one of the most recognized leaders of civil rights for African Americans was an ordained Christian minister, Frederick Douglass. A gifted orator, Douglass was a key counselor on civil rights and voting rights to Presidents Abraham Lincoln and Ulysses S. Grant.

One hundred years later, the movements for civil and voting rights were blessed again with another leader, also an ordained Christian minister and

---

[304] https://www.britannica.com/topic/civil-rights.

gifted orator, Dr. Martin Luther King Jr. Like Frederick Douglass, Dr. King was a key counselor to a president, Lyndon B. Johnson.

Evangelical Christians, both black and white, fought side by side to realize that "arrival of freedom," which my friend David Barton of WallBuilders speaks about in the opening of this chapter. Their sacrifices were rewarded with the trilogy of changes to the Constitution that guaranteed the abolishment of slavery, the rights of citizenship, and the right to vote. Bible-believing Christians applauded this arrival of freedom as an example of good defeating evil.

However, there were other powerful forces who wanted to recreate a slave-like atmosphere in the South. Sadly, often under the guise of religion, they utilized methods and tactics that true Christians should deem only as evil. An article from the *National Black Robe Regiment* lists many of these ugly methods and tactics:

> Many states condoned violence from White supremacist groups like the Ku Klux Klan (KKK) and devised poll taxes, literacy tests, "Jim Crow" laws, "Black Codes," the "One-Drop Rule" and other similar legal constructs to keep Black Americans disenfranchised.[305]

It is politically painful, as truth often is, but history records every one of these actions as closely planned, managed, and executed by the Democratic Party.

So who was considered the first civil rights president?

President Abraham Lincoln, the first Republican president, is a great answer. However, he is not the correct response.

But never forget the political sacrifices of Abraham Lincoln. He worked with abolitionist Frederick Douglass to issue his Emancipation Proclamation. Lincoln risked his 1864 reelection by demanding the passage of the

---

[305] https://nationalblackroberegiment.com/july-2-1864-july-2-1964-july-2-2014/.

Thirteenth Amendment, the permanent abolition of slavery in all states and territories, be included in the Republican platform.

Andrew Johnson, the Democrat who was sworn in as president after the assassination of Abraham Lincoln, is a bad response. In 1866 he vetoed the first civil rights legislation of Congress. In a historic milestone, the House overrode President Andrew Johnson's veto of the Civil Rights Bill of 1866 with near unanimous Republican support, 122 to 41.[306]

One hundred years later, Lyndon B. Johnson was sworn in as president after the assassination of John F. Kennedy. President Johnson, a Democrat, is an awesome answer. However, he is not the correct answer.

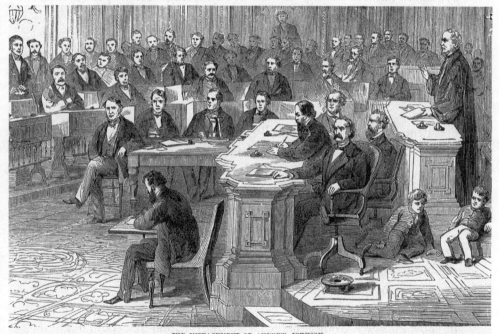

THE IMPEACHMENT OF ANDREW JOHNSON.

The 1868 impeachment of 17th President, Andrew Johnson.

---

[306] https://history.house.gov/Historical-Highlights/1851-1900/The-Civil-Rights-Bill-of-1866/.

The iconic photos of President Johnson with Dr. King at the signing of both the 1964 civil rights bill and the 1965 voting rights bill are historic memories.

The Civil Rights Act of 1964 was most significant civil rights legislation passed since Reconstruction. The act outlawed discrimination based on race, color, religion, sex, or national origin. Also prohibited were the unequal application of voter registration requirements and racial segregation in schools.[307] Dr. Martin Luther King Jr. referred to it as the "Second Emancipation Proclamation."[308]

The signing of the act was a nationally televised event, with President Lyndon B. Johnson stating, "Let us close the springs of racial poison," and "Let us lay aside irrelevant differences and make our Nation whole."[309]

Recognizing his work on the Civil Rights Act of 1964, Dr. Martin Luther King Jr., at age thirty-five, became the youngest recipient of the Noble Peace Prize.[310]

President Lyndon B. Johnson also signed into law the Voting Rights Act of 1965. Since Reconstruction there were legal barriers, especially in the South, to the Fifteenth Amendment's constitutional right to vote for African Americans. Discriminatory voting practices including literacy tests were outlawed.[311]

Answer: The answer to this *Mercer Moment in American History* is D, the eighteenth president, Ulysses S. Grant. President Grant is considered our first civil rights president.

In 1869, President Grant inherited a wounded nation that could not heal under former President Andrew Johnson. President Johnson was a barrier

---

[307] https://nationalblackroberegiment.com/july-2-1864-july-2-1964-july-2-2014/.

[308] https://nationalblackroberegiment.com/july-2-1864-july-2-1964-july-2-2014/.

[309] https://history.house.gov/Historical-Highlights/1951-2000/The-Civil-Rights-Act-of-1964/.

[310] https://wallbuilders.com/martin-luther-king-jr/#_ftn3.

[311] https://www.history.com/topics/black-history/voting-rights-act.

against the Reconstruction of the South and opposed the new rights of citizenship to the newly freed African Americans.[312]

Beginning four years before Grant's inauguration, the newly formed Ku Klux Klan (KKK) began terrorizing and murdering thousands of former slaves and their sympathetic white Southern Republican supporters. Among other things, the KKK opposed the rights of newly freed slaves to vote, run for office, or serve on juries.

For example, in July 1866, black and white delegates attended the Constitution Convention for Louisiana. The delegates proudly marched with the Union flag to their meeting only to be blocked by the mayor of New Orleans and a racist mob of white supremacists.[313]

In what is now known as the New Orleans Massacre, or the New Orleans Race Riots, shots were fired at unarmed marchers that first day, killing thirty-seven blacks and three whites who allied with black suffrage. One report states that over two hundred more blacks were murdered in the days that followed.[314], [315]

Northern Christian groups and abolitionists were outraged at the extreme violence and senseless murders. The images of the viciousness of the riots impacted the congressional elections of 1866. The Republican Party took majority control of the US House of Representatives and the US Senate.[316]

---

[312] https://www.history.com/news/ulysses-s-grant-president-accomplishments-scandals-15th-amendment.

[313] https://www.blackpast.org/african-american-history/new-orleans-massacre-1866/.

[314] https://www.pbs.org/wgbh/americanexperience/features/grant-kkk/?flavour=mobile.

[315] https://www.blackpast.org/african-american-history/new-orleans-massacre-1866/.

[316] https://www.blackpast.org/african-american-history/new-orleans-massacre-1866/.

*President Ulysses S. Grant sitting at the center of a large
table, signing the 15th amendment, granting that the
right to vote cannot be denied on basis of race or color. The
amendment granted African-American men the right to vote
and was adopted into the U.S. Constitution in 1870.*

In his 1869 inaugural address, President Ulysses S. Grant strongly advocated for the states to ratify the Fifteenth Amendment to our Constitution. He wanted to end the disenfranchisement of African American men and guarantee their right to vote.[317] In March of 1869, his first year in office, President Grant signed into law protections for the equal rights for blacks to serve on juries and hold office.

President Grant then created the Department of Justice (DOJ). His attorney general and the new position of solicitor general now had the federal power to prosecute the KKK. The DOJ was successful in securing thousands of federal indictments again the leaders of the KKK.

In 1871, Grant led passage and then signed the Ku Klux Klan Act, which gave the president the power to declare martial law in those states with the worst levels of violence and murder against the new Republican voters and their supporters. By then, Southern Democrats and the KKK had increased intimidation and horrific violence to prevent newly freed African Americans from registering to vote and then voting as Republicans.[318]

President Grant sent federal troops to South Carolina and other parts of the South to protect both the registration of new voters and their casting of ballots. The Ku Klux Klan Act, coupled with President Grant's new DOJ, defeated the hooded terrorists, who went into hiding and would not reappear in force until the 1910s.[319]

Frederick Douglass gave these remarks after President Ulysses S. Grant died:

> To him, more than to any other man, the Negro owes his enfranchisement.

---

[317] https://www.history.com/news/ulysses-s-grant-president-accomplishments-scandals-15th-amendment.

[318] https://www.history.com/topics/us-presidents/ulysses-s-grant-1.

[319] https://www.history.com/topics/us-presidents/ulysses-s-grant-1.

When red-handed violence ran rampant through the South, and freedmen were being hunted down like wild beasts in the night, the moral courage and fidelity of Gen. Grant transcended that of his party.[320]

I agree with Ron Chernow, who wrote that "Grant deserves an honored place in American history, second only to Lincoln, for what he did for the freed slaves."[321]

---

[320] https://www.history.com/news/ulysses-s-grant-president-accomplishments-scandals-15th-amendment.

[321] https://www.history.com/news/ulysses-s-grant-president-accomplishments-scandals-15th-amendment.

Today there are over 40 million human slaves. There are more slaves today than at any other time in our world.

Epilogue

Human slavery is evil. Slaves first arrived in North America in 1619. However, too many American students now believe this false theory: America invented slavery and worldwide slavery began in 1619.

Our schools are filled with a divisive, political agenda of the "1619 Project" and the "Critical Race Theory." The intent of this book, *Slavery 101*, is to provide a historically fair and accurate response to unite America by documenting the profound impact and milestones of "The Great Awakening."

In 2002, I was elected to Texas' State Legislature and until 2020 to the State Board of Education. I labored for hundreds of hours with my colleagues at meetings, hearing public testimony and doing personal research. We developed history standards and curriculum for students.

I successfully advanced forgotten African American heroes including Rev. Hiram Revels, Wentworth Cheswell, and Sgt. William Carney. Though we prevailed, many "experts" resisted studying more of Frederick Douglass, and the contributions of anti-slavery leaders William Wilberforce and John Quincy Adams.

Before 1776, not one nation in the world had abolished slavery. The Arab-Muslim slave trade began after 700 AD, 750 years before Columbus discovered the New World and 1000 years before our 1776 Declaration of Independence.

In our 21st Century, it is estimated that every 30 seconds another human being is forced to become a slave.

In the 18th and 19th centuries, a new breed of American and British Christians "woke up" and joined together to fight against an 8,000-year-old, powerful evil to defeat the sin of global human slavery.

That Great Awakening resulted in the movement of a Christian evangelical army to abolish slavery. The impact of revival began with the United States and the United Kingdom, and then it spread to the entire world.

In the United Kingdom, for Christian abolitionists, the "fruits of their labor" became the 1807 law to abolish the international slave trade and then Parliament's 1833 act to abolish all slavery.

In the United States, those "fruits" began with the seeds planted in our Declaration of Independence and in our original Constitution.

Our Emancipation Proclamation, three post-Civil War Constitutional Amendments, the creation of the Department of Justice, and the Civil Rights Act of 1866 are a few of the many historical events documented in this book. Each were championed by Christians committed by their faith to stand firm against the powerful, political, and financial forces of worldwide slavery.

Because of the efforts led by many committed Christians, African American men were finally allowed to vote in 1870.

Before 1870, contrary to the agenda of those promoting today's Critical Race Theory, Christians from our historical past fervently convinced Anglo American voters from three-fourths of the 1865-1869 states to ratify a trilogy of constitutional amendments.

For the record, these were three separate amendments voted on and ratified in three different years to: abolish slavery (1865), declare rights of citizenship (1866), and grant the right to vote (1869).

I remind my American brothers and sisters that we may win a major battle, but the war against evil never ends.

Too often in history (and in our present day), efforts against slavery were hindered by weak politicians who did not have the courage to get involved in the discussion, debate, and abolition of slavery.

Finally, having shared so much in this book "Slavery 101," I must warn all Christians never to become what I call a Christian "sognog." "Sog" meaning "so good" and "nog" meaning "no good." We must not become "sognogs" like the New Testament Pharisees where they became "so good" that they were "no good." We must not become so heavenly minded that we are no earthly good!

Why? Today, there are more human slaves than at any time in our world's history. Each night, over 40 million children, women, and men cry out for a "Moses" to deliver them soon, very soon.

Christians are once again called to unite for a "21st Century Great Awakening." Men and women of faith, this is a "shout out" to "Ephesians 6" for us to rise-up and make a difference in our world.

I challenge the Church to wake up, unite, and answer that call for a 21st Century Moses.

As always,
Amen. Amen. Alleluia. Amen.

Appendix A

Romans Road to Salvation

We are all sinners
Romans 3:23
For all have sinned and fall short of the glory of God.

Eternal life is a free gift
Romans 6:23
**For the wages of sin is death, but the gift of God
is eternal life in Christ Jesus our Lord.**

God demonstrated His love for us
Romans 5:8
**But God demonstrates his own love for us in this:
While we were still sinners, Christ died for us.**

You must trust and surrender to Jesus as your Lord
Romans 10:9-10
**If you declare with your mouth, "Jesus is Lord,"
and believe in your heart that God raised him from the dead,
you will be saved.
For it is with your heart that you believe
and are justified, and it is with your mouth
that you profess your faith and are saved.**

Your assurance is through Jesus
Romans 10:13
Everyone who calls on the name of the Lord will be saved.

Appendix B

Selected Excerpts from the US Constitution

We the People of the United States, in Order to form a more perfect Union, establish Justice, insure domestic Tranquility, provide for the common defence, promote the general Welfare, and secure the Blessings of Liberty to ourselves and our Posterity, do ordain and establish this Constitution for the United States of America.

Article I

Section 2: The House of Representatives

The House of Representatives shall be composed of Members chosen every second Year by the People of the several States, and the Electors in each State shall have the Qualifications requisite for Electors of the most numerous Branch of the State Legislature.

No Person shall be a Representative who shall not have attained to the Age of twenty five Years, and been seven Years a Citizen of the United States, and who shall not, when elected, be an Inhabitant of that State in which he shall be chosen.

Representatives and direct Taxes shall be apportioned among the several States which may be included within this Union, according to their respective Numbers, which shall be determined by adding to the whole Number of free Persons, including those bound to Service for a Term of

Years, and excluding Indians not taxed, three fifths of all other Persons. The actual Enumeration shall be made within three Years after the first Meeting of the Congress of the United States, and within every subsequent Term of ten Years, in such Manner as they shall by Law direct.The number of Representatives shall not exceed one for every thirty Thousand, but each State shall have at Least one Representative; and until such enumeration shall be made, the State of New Hampshire shall be entitled to chuse three, Massachusetts eight, Rhode-Island and Providence Plantations one, Connecticut five, New-York six, New Jersey four, Pennsylvania eight, Delaware one, Maryland six, Virginia ten, North Carolina five, South Carolina five, and Georgia three.

When vacancies happen in the Representation from any State, the Executive Authority thereof shall issue Writs of Election to fill such Vacancies.

The House of Representatives shall chuse their Speaker and other Officers;and shall have the sole Power of Impeachment.

Section 3: The Senate

The Senate of the United States shall be composed of two Senators from each State, chosen by the Legislature thereof, for six Years; and each Senator shall have one Vote.

Immediately after they shall be assembled in Consequence of the first Election, they shall be divided as equally as may be into three Classes. The Seats of the Senators of the first Class shall be vacated at the Expiration of the second Year, of the second Class at the Expiration of the fourth Year, and of the third Class at the Expiration of the sixth Year, so that one third may be chosen every second Year; and if Vacancies happen by Resignation, or otherwise, during the Recess of the Legislature of any State, the Executive thereof may make temporary Appointments until the next Meeting of the Legislature, which shall then fill such Vacancies.

No Person shall be a Senator who shall not have attained to the Age of thirty Years, and been nine Years a Citizen of the United States, and who shall not, when elected, be an Inhabitant of that State for which he shall be chosen.

The Vice President of the United States shall be President of the Senate, but shall have no Vote, unless they be equally divided.

The Senate shall chuse their other Officers, and also a President pro tempore, in the Absence of the Vice President, or when he shall exercise the Office of President of the United States.

The Senate shall have the sole Power to try all Impeachments. When sitting for that Purpose, they shall be on Oath or Affirmation. When the President of the United States is tried, the Chief Justice shall preside: And no Person shall be convicted without the Concurrence of two thirds of the Members present.

Judgment in Cases of Impeachment shall not extend further than to removal from Office, and disqualification to hold and enjoy any Office of honor, Trust or Profit under the United States: but the Party convicted shall nevertheless be liable and subject to Indictment, Trial, Judgment and Punishment, according to Law.

Section 9: Powers Denied Congress

The Migration or Importation of such Persons as any of the States now existing shall think proper to admit, shall not be prohibited by the Congress prior to the Year one thousand eight hundred and eight, but a Tax or duty may be imposed on such Importation, not exceeding ten dollars for each Person.

The Privilege of the Writ of Habeas Corpus shall not be suspended, unless when in Cases of Rebellion or Invasion the public Safety may require it.

No Bill of Attainder or ex post facto Law shall be passed.

No Capitation, or other direct, Tax shall be laid, unless in Proportion to the Census or Enumeration herein before directed to be taken.

No Tax or Duty shall be laid on Articles exported from any State.

No Preference shall be given by any Regulation of Commerce or Revenue to the Ports of one State over those of another: nor shall Vessels bound to, or from, one State, be obliged to enter, clear, or pay Duties in another.

No Money shall be drawn from the Treasury, but in Consequence of Appropriations made by Law; and a regular Statement and Account of the Receipts and Expenditures of all public Money shall be published from time to time.

No Title of Nobility shall be granted by the United States: And no Person holding any Office of Profit or Trust under them, shall, without the Consent of the Congress, accept of any present, Emolument, Office, or Title, of any kind whatever, from any King, Prince, or foreign State.

Article V

The Congress, whenever two thirds of both Houses shall deem it necessary, shall propose Amendments to this Constitution, or, on the Application of the Legislatures of two thirds of the several States, shall call a Convention for proposing Amendments, which, in either Case, shall be valid to all Intents and Purposes, as Part of this Constitution, when ratified by the Legislatures of three fourths of the several States, or by Conventions in three fourths thereof, as the one or the other Mode of Ratification may be proposed by the Congress; Provided that no Amendment which may be made prior to the Year One thousand eight hundred and eight shall in any Manner affect the first and fourth Clauses in the Ninth Section of the first Article; and that no State, without its Consent, shall be deprived of its equal Suffrage in the Senate.

First Amendment

Congress shall make no law respecting an establishment of religion, or prohibiting the free exercise thereof; or abridging the freedom of speech, or of the press; or the right of the people peaceably to assemble, and to petition the Government for a redress of grievances.

Second Amendment

A well regulated Militia, being necessary to the security of a free State, the right of the people to keep and bear Arms, shall not be infringed.

Third Amendment

No Soldier shall, in time of peace be quartered in any house, without the consent of the Owner, nor in time of war, but in a manner to be prescribed by law.

Fourth Amendment

The right of the people to be secure in their persons, houses, papers, and effects, against unreasonable searches and seizures, shall not be violated, and no Warrants shall issue, but upon probable cause, supported by Oath or affirmation, and particularly describing the place to be searched, and the persons or things to be seized.

Fifth Amendment

No person shall be held to answer for a capital, or otherwise infamous crime, unless on a presentment or indictment of a Grand Jury, except in cases arising in the land or naval forces, or in the Militia, when in actual service in time of War or public danger; nor shall any person be subject for the same offence to be twice put in jeopardy of life or limb; nor shall be compelled in any criminal case to be a witness against himself, nor be deprived of life, liberty, or property, without due process of law; nor shall private property be taken for public use, without just compensation.

Sixth Amendment

In all criminal prosecutions, the accused shall enjoy the right to a speedy and public trial, by an impartial jury of the State and district wherein the crime shall have been committed, which district shall have been previously ascertained by law, and to be informed of the nature and cause of the accusation; to be confronted with the witnesses against him; to have compulsory process for obtaining witnesses in his favor, and to have the Assistance of Counsel for his defence.

Seventh Amendment

In Suits at common law, where the value in controversy shall exceed twenty dollars, the right of trial by jury shall be preserved, and no fact tried by a jury, shall be otherwise reexamined in any Court of the United States, than according to the rules of the common law.

Eighth Amendment

Excessive bail shall not be required, nor excessive fines imposed, nor cruel and unusual punishments inflicted.

Ninth Amendment

The enumeration in the Constitution, of certain rights, shall not be construed to deny or disparage others retained by the people.

10th Amendment

The powers not delegated to the United States by the Constitution, nor prohibited by it to the States, are reserved to the States respectively, or to the people.

13th Amendment

Section 1

Neither slavery nor involuntary servitude, except as a punishment for crime whereof the party shall have been duly convicted, shall exist within the United States, or any place subject to their jurisdiction.

Section 2

Congress shall have power to enforce this article by appropriate legislation.

14th Amendment

Section 1

All persons born or naturalized in the United States, and subject to the jurisdiction thereof, are citizens of the United States and of the State wherein they reside. No State shall make or enforce any law which shall abridge the privileges or immunities of citizens of the United States; nor shall any State deprive any person of life, liberty, or property, without due process of law; nor deny to any person within its jurisdiction the equal protection of the laws.

Section 2

Representatives shall be apportioned among the several States according to their respective numbers, counting the whole number of persons in each State, excluding Indians not taxed. But when the right to vote at any election for the choice of electors for President and Vice-President of the United States, Representatives in Congress, the Executive and Judicial officers of a State, or the members of the Legislature thereof, is denied to any of the male inhabitants of such State, being twenty-one years of age, and citizens of the United States, or in any way abridged, except for participation in rebellion, or other crime, the basis of representation therein shall be reduced in the proportion which the number of such male citizens shall bear to the whole number of male citizens twenty-one years of age in such State.

Section 3

No person shall be a Senator or Representative in Congress, or elector of President and Vice-President, or hold any office, civil or military, under the United States, or under any State, who, having previously taken an oath, as a member of Congress, or as an officer of the United States, or as a member of any State legislature, or as an executive or judicial officer of any State, to support the Constitution of the United States, shall have engaged in insurrection or rebellion against the same, or given aid or comfort to the enemies thereof. But Congress may by a vote of two-thirds of each House, remove such disability.

Section 4

The validity of the public debt of the United States, authorized by law, including debts incurred for payment of pensions and bounties for services in suppressing insurrection or rebellion, shall not be questioned. But neither the United States nor any State shall assume or pay any debt or obligation incurred in aid of insurrection or rebellion against the United States, or any claim for the loss or emancipation of any slave; but all such debts, obligations and claims shall be held illegal and void.

Section 5

The Congress shall have the power to enforce, by appropriate legislation, the provisions of this article.

15th Amendment

Section 1

The right of citizens of the United States to vote shall not be denied or abridged by the United States or by any State on account of race, color, or previous condition of servitude.

Section 2

The Congress shall have the power to enforce this article by appropriate legislation.

17th Amendment

The Senate of the United States shall be composed of two Senators from each State, elected by the people thereof, for six years; and each Senator shall have one vote. The electors in each State shall have the qualifications requisite for electors of the most numerous branch of the State legislatures.

When vacancies happen in the representation of any State in the Senate, the executive authority of such State shall issue writs of election to fill such vacancies: Provided, That the legislature of any State may empower the executive thereof to make temporary appointments until the people fill the vacancies by election as the legislature may direct.

This amendment shall not be so construed as to affect the election or term of any Senator chosen before it becomes valid as part of the Constitution.

19th Amendment

The right of citizens of the United States to vote shall not be denied or abridged by the United States or by any State on account of sex.

Congress shall have power to enforce this article by appropriate legislation.

Index